Dropshipping Shopify E-Commerce 2019:

A Step by Step Guide on How to Make $10,000/Month Online with SEO, Social Media Marketing, Blogging and instagram

By

William Devine

This book is copyright (c) 2019 by **William Devine**

All rights are reserved. This book may not be duplicated or copied, either in whole or in part, via any means including any electronic form of duplication such as recording or transcription. The contents of this book may not be transmitted, stored in any retrieval system, or copied in any other manner regardless of whether use is public or private without express prior permission of the publisher. This book provides information only. The author does not offer any specific advice, including medical advice, nor does the author suggest the reader or any other person engage in any particular course of conduct in any specific situation. This book is not intended to be used as a substitute for any professional advice, medical or of any other variety. The reader accepts sole responsibility for how he or she uses the information contained in this book. Under no circumstances will the publisher or the author be held liable for damages of any kind arising either directly or indirectly from any information contained in this book.

TABLE OF CONTENTS

INTRODUCTION 5

    What is Drop Shipping? 6

    Pros and Cons Of DropShipping 7

    Things to do before starting dropshipping 15

    Why you should start a Dropshipping Business 17

    Start With Your Big WHY, Which Is Your Big Goal And Dream. A Success Mindset Of Dropshipping 21

    Getting Started In Online Drop Shipping 24

        Select a Niche 24

        Select a Profitable Product 34

        Finding a Dropshipping Supplier 39

        Choose the Best Dropshipping Platform 59

        Types of dropshipping platforms 60

    Factors to Evaluate When Choosing a Dropshipping Platform 64

    Top Ecommerce Platforms For Dropshipping Businesses? 67

    Building a Successful e-commerce Business .. 77

    Build a Blog That is Optimized for Search Engines 78

    Create an Ecommerce Marketing Strategy 83

TAX ID and taxes 91

Right Pricing: Pricing Strategy To Stay Two Steps Ahead Of Your Competitors 94

Product Descriptions 100

$10,000/Month Strategies: Dropshipping Secrets To Success 104

How to Start Dropshipping With Shopify 129

How To Start Dropshipping With Amazon 171

How To Start Dropshipping With Ebay 176

How To Promote Your Brand And Your Products 184

How to Use SEO to Skyrocket Your Business Growth 191

What Is SEO 191

How to Handle Security Issues with your business 196

How to handle Your customers and provide Exemplary Customer Services 203

Ways to Get Your Startup Funded 207

How Much Do Dropshippers Make And How Soon 212

Reasons of Dropshipping Failures 215

Dropshipping Mistakes to Avoid 220

Dropshipping Tips To Skyrocket Your Sales in 2019 222

Frequently Asked Question 234

CONCLUSION 242

Summary 242

INTRODUCTION

The popularity of drop shipping has grown significantly over the last decade with the proliferation of retail stores online. Drop shipping is considered a best practice in just-in-time inventory management and supply chain management where the retailer does not keep any merchandise in stock. Instead, customer orders are sent to either the manufacturer or to a wholesaler that then ships the items directly to the customer. Drop shipping is commonly used by catalog, mail order, and internet retail businesses to offer the customer a wide variety of items without making an investment in inventory.

Drop shipping is good business for manufacturers, distributors and retailers. Suppliers concentrate on manufacturing and shipping, while the retailer concentrates on sales and customer service - each to his own talents. Duplication of effort in the supply chain is reduced along with related costs as only one member in the chain needs to 'pick, pack and ship'. Drop shipping is also good for the consumer as savings in warehousing and shipping costs can be passed on by the retailer.

WHAT IS DROP SHIPPING?

Well, this form of online retailing is when you list an item, on eBay or Amazon for example, without having the product in inventory. You generally work with a wholesaler, advertise their product at retail price, and when a customer purchases the aforementioned item, you order the product. Usually and profitably you purchase the item from a wholesaler at a discounted price. At this point the wholesaler, usually for free, ships the neatly packaged, new and impeccable, item directly to your buyer. You are essentially Walmart, with less less fluorescent lights and better fashion taste.

You have no overhead, no risk, and no inventory except virtually. Best of all, you never even have to exhume your old printer from the basement to print postage labels. It sounds illegal but its not, and technically not even unethical. Retail stores do it. You spend the time researching and advertising, surely it is only fair you that you get your cut of the profits. The wholesaler is happy as his sales skyrocket and your customer is happy as they receive a professionally packaged brand new item directly to their door. You are happy as you slowly watch that $100 you had put away for that trip to the casino turn into $1000 virtually in a couple weeks.

PROS AND CONS OF DROPSHIPPING

Here are pros and cons of dropshipping

Pros

If you're planning to start an online retail business, drop shipping may be just the option for you.

Let's review the process of drop shipping, and analyze the advantages that the drop shipping business model has over the others.

No Upfront Payment

First of all, you do not need to pay upfront for a stock of products before you can start selling. With drop shipping, you can simply get into business by displaying the products you want to sell on your website, before you've actually purchased any of the goods. After you've received your order via the internet, you can then forward the order to the drop shipper, usually through email, who will then deliver the products to your customer(s).

In essence, this is the reverse process of normal retailers. You actually 'sell high' first before 'buying low'. Since you're not making a huge upfront down-payment for your products, you're not bearing any risk at all. There isn't a risk of purchasing thousands of units of a product, and realizing that you're not able to sell them because the consumer demand is insufficient.

Thus, by not needing to make an upfront payment to stock products, you're benefiting in two ways. One, the drop shipper bears all the risk for you. If the products are not in-demand, it's the drop shipper who is potentially making a loss, not you. Second, your startup costs are extremely low. All you need to invest in your drop shipping business is an initial deposit or down-payment, to demonstrate your commitment to the drop shipper, and also ongoing web hosting fees and advertising fees. This is a huge difference from retailers who have to invest on a fortune to purchase huge stocks of goods to get into business.

Product Delivery Taken Care Of

The second feature of drop shippers is that they take care of the products delivery and shipment for you. This is highly advantageous if you're just starting out in business because you can focus all your time and efforts on marketing your business, instead of worrying about order fulfillment or delivery.

Order fulfillment can be a very tedious and time-consuming process if your monthly orders number in the hundreds or thousands. You need to spend tremendous amounts of time keeping track of your inventory, packaging the products and shipping them to your customers individually. On the other hand, if a drop shipper takes care of product fulfillment for you, you're automating the process of shipping the products, and you can focus on your core competency - marketing your business to bring in more customers. This is another great advantage of using drop shipping as your business model.

No Need For Warehousing

Since you do not need to purchase a huge inventory of stocks from the drop shipper, there's no need for warehousing costs as well.

This is highly advantageous if you consider this opposite scenario: If you rely on the usual wholesaling business model instead of drop shipping, you need a location to store your products after purchasing your initial stock. Depending on the space you need, your monthly warehouse rental costs can cut into your profit margin significantly. You may even be operating your business at a loss. Why not let the drop shipper stock the products at their warehouse until your customer makes a purchase instead?

Flexibility Of Product Catalogue

With drop shipping, you have the choice of promoting any number of products you want on your website catalogue. Since you do not need to make upfront capital investments, you have the flexibility of promoting as many products as you want, as long as the products are all related to the category of products you sell.

However, it's essential to strike a balance between the range of products you have, and the 'product focus' of your business. Your business should focus on a single category of products - you cannot be a supplier of everything to everyone, like Wal-Mart. Be sure to include only the products you think are related to your core 'product focus', and avoid promoting too many unrelated products on your web catalogue.

No Minimum Quantity Restriction

The last advantage of drop shipping is that most drop shippers do not impose a minimum quantity order. When your customers place orders at your website, you can forward your orders to your drop shipper one-by-one. Most drop shippers do not have a problem with that. Thus, drop shipping is very beneficial for your business because it offers the greatest flexibility.

Cons

At this point, running a drop shipping business probably seems like an attractive option. But be aware that there are also disadvantages to this business model that you should consider before getting started.

Retailer Liability For Supplier Errors

Another downside to being a dropship retailer relates to liability for supplier errors. Under the dropship model, the customer buys directly from the retailer without ever interacting with the supplier. As far as the customer is concerned, the entire transaction occurs on the retailer's website, meaning that the retailer will always bear complete responsibility and necessarily accept fault for any packaging or shipping errors on the part of the supplier. Because it will always be the retailer's reputation at stake, it's crucial that as a retailer, you work exclusively with experienced and high-quality suppliers.

Inventory Management Issues

Building on the last point, it's worth discussing the complications of inventory management, which can sometimes create huge headaches for retailers. As a dropship retailer, you neither own nor stock the items that you sell. Because you're sourcing these products from a variety of suppliers, who themselves are fulfilling orders for a variety of other retailers, you can expect supplier inventory to fluctuate daily, and tracking these changes can be very difficult.

While software does exist to monitor the warehouse stock of your suppliers, this technology is expensive, not always accurate, and in some cases not supported by your supplier of choice. System errors or miscommunications can give rise to problems that force you to cancel an order or place it on backorder. Again, as the retailer, you will bear full liability for these mishaps.

Highly Competitive

A low barrier to entry means high competition. It is precisely because of the advantages of the drop shipping model that competition is high: because virtually anyone with a laptop and wifi connection can operate an online drop shipping store at a very low cost, this has become a popular option for online retailers, causing many markets to become oversaturated with merchants offering very low-priced products. The best way to avoid this problem, especially for new businesses, is to conduct adequate market research to better understand which niche markets and segments are less crowded, and therefore afford you an opportunity to establish and distinguish yourself without getting lost in a sea of competitors.

Minimal Brand Control

In the ecommerce world, where businesses are already somewhat estranged from their customers, the personalized details of an order can make a huge difference in building customer satisfaction and brand loyalty. Unfortunately, however, when you entrust a drop shipping supplier with the task of filling, packaging, and shipping your orders, you lose control over product presentation. Because drop shipping suppliers are filling huge numbers of orders from multiple sources daily, there simply isn't the time or incentive to include personalized packaging or customized notes with customer orders. Those suppliers that are willing to package orders with your logo will charge a pretty penny for that service. The benefit of offloading order fulfilment onto someone else comes at the cost of entrusting your brand's reputation to a third party. (Yet another reason to choose your suppliers wisely; more on this below.)

If your main goal is to build your reputation and grow brand recognition, then drop shipping is probably not the best business model for you.

Low Profit Margins

The profit you make as a drop shipping business is the difference between what your customer pays you for a product and what you pay your drop shipping supplier to ship that product to your customer. Because drop shipping is such a competitive industry, this profit margin can often be pretty small, especially if you sell high-end niche items that are expensive to buy from suppliers.

While it's unlikely you'll ever make a 100% profit using the drop shipping model, you can best maximize your profit margins by choosing a market segment that is well-suited for the dropship model and finding suppliers with fair prices.

THINGS TO DO BEFORE STARTING DROPSHIPPING

There are i's to dot and t's to cross when setting up dropshipping.

Legal requirements for running a dropshipping company vary from state to state, let alone country to country, so check, check and check again that your site is compliant. It could save you trouble further down the line. And remember, laws change all the time so stay on top of things like filing your annual report to make sure once you're compliant you stay that way.

Most genuine wholesalers and manufacturers won't work with you unless you can provide your EIN (Employment Identification Number). If you pay tax – one of life's certainties – you need one of these. Even if you don't have any employees, you need to have one.

Getting an EIN is also really handy for keeping personal and business taxes and finances separate. They're simple and inexpensive to get hold of – just apply on the IRS website.

Registering your business name and domain name with the relevant authorities will protect your distinct company name from being copied. The Small Business Administration has excellent advice on setting up companies in America.

It's very important you get proper counsel if you're unsure of the boxes you need to tick to run your dropshipping business.

WHY YOU SHOULD START A DROPSHIPPING BUSINESS

Of all of the possibilities for running an e-commerce website, one with a dropshipping business model is perhaps the most enticing.

Just like any small business, an online e-commerce business certainly has its pros and cons. The difference is that many of the cons that come with running a dropshipping company will come with running any online store, making the dropshipping business model one with lots of unique benefits.

Some of the most notable benefits are listed here.

Customizable Profit Margins

Because you don't pay for packaging, stock the product, or manufacture anything, your costs are super low, relative to other small business models. You simply cover the cost of the wholesale price and collect the rest. That means that there is tremendous opportunity for decent profit margins on all of your products.

More Free Time

While there will certainly be periods of full-time work required to get your online e-commerce business up and running, running a dropshipping site often feels more like a part-time job with super flexible hours than a traditional 9 to 5 job.

Aside from working with your customers in the event that they run into problems or coordinating with your shipping suppliers from time to time, the time commitment of running a dropshipping site is pretty minimal.

This is where the term 'passive income' comes from and why it is so popular among budding entrepreneurs. Income can be earned with (relatively) minimal effort with a dropshipping business model.

More Flexibility in The Market

Things happen. Trends come and go, the economy crashes, and advancing technology changes the way people purchase products. The dropshipping business model allows you the flexibility to pivot when these otherwise devastating shifts happen in the market. You can follow in real-time which trending products are the most profitable and which are cutting into your profit margins the most.

Then, depending on where the trends are headed, you can adjust your focus accordingly with very little risk.

Very few business models allow for this much flexibility, especially without costing the business a pretty penny to pivot in an ever-changing market.

Low Costs

The dropshipping business model requires very little money to start selling and earning money.

In fact, you could start your business for just the cost of running your website, if you wanted to.

Whatever costs come with opening a drop shipping store are virtually negligible compared to any other small business start-up costs.

How?

You are not producing any products, purchasing any materials, or paying any operational costs. Virtually the only thing that you need to pay for when you run a dropshipping company is the website from which you sell your products and any ads that you place.

Can Be Managed From Anywhere

Perhaps the most desirable benefits of running a dropshipping business are the kind of personal freedom that comes with it. The only thing you need to run an e-commerce website is a solid internet connection and a computer to work from.

And that is a pretty easy list to fulfill from virtually anywhere in the world.

START WITH YOUR BIG WHY, WHICH IS YOUR BIG GOAL AND DREAM. A SUCCESS MINDSET OF DROPSHIPPING

Starting your own dropshipping business can be exhilarating. There's nothing like the possibility of earning a steady income from dropshipping to motivate you at first.

The thing is, if you fail, it can be costly—lost time, lost money, lost self-esteem.

The Ultimate Mindset for Dropshipping – The Bad Mindset

With a bad mindset you will be afraid to spend money on testing and acquiring data. As I said before, you may "hit a home run" with your first product or you may not. For most people it will probably require some testing before finding the "home run" product. To find this product you must be willing to swing and be unafraid of missing. When you test a product and learn from it, you are becoming a better marketer by understanding what your audience likes and does not. When you spend money on Facebook ads, you are learning new tactics and acquiring new data for your pixel. The more data your pixel acquires the more optimized it will become. This will increase the chances of Facebook finding your ideal customer which will increase your sales dramatically.

Your first dropshipping idea may not be the best idea. You may choose an unprofitable niche. It's important to remember your chances of succeeding with your second store will be much higher. This is because you will have learned so much from your first store which can be used to improve the second one. If you remember what I said about finding a profitable niche then this shouldn't be a problem. If you have forgotten, I'll refresh your memory quickly. They should have a relatively high income, they should be passionate about the subject and they should be on the advertising platform. If you follow those three rules then it's hard to go wrong.

The Ultimate Mindset for Dropshipping – The Winning Mindset

A winning mindset will ensure you are not afraid to fail. When you fail, you learn. Every mistake you made can be adapted and thus applied to your next venture. A good mindset will mean you view failure as an opportunity for success. You should not be afraid to spend money on Facebook advertising. Dropshipping is inexpensive to begin but you must be willing to part with some money. View this as a learning experience. You are collecting valuable data to allow your Facebook pixel to optimize and target the perfect customer. There are over two billion people on Facebook and it can be difficult to find the right people for your store. Spending money will increase the likelihood that you find these people.

Dropshipping requires you to be constantly testing new products. You must go into this process with an open mind. Every product will not be a "home run" but you need to go through many products to find these. If you are not prepared to test multiple products then you probably won't find these home runs.

I want you to commit to having the ultimate mindset for dropshipping. This will increase your chances of succeeding with dropshipping dramatically. View every failure as a learning experience instead of a disaster. These are often the times when the "eureka moment" hits us. It is a natural process every new business must go through.

GETTING STARTED IN ONLINE DROP SHIPPING

There are three key elements to address as you create your e-business plan in preparation to earn extra money drop shipping.

- Decide what types of products you want to sell
- Sourcing these products, which means locating reliable vendors for the items that you want to sell
- Building not only a website but building a successful e-commerce business!

SELECT A NICHE

As tempting as it may be to jump into the biggest global trends, it's best to hang back and focus on smaller trends, instead.

Why?

Because major brands with major marketing budgets will likely be selling globally trending products, making it nearly impossible for you to compete with.

Rather than competing with these multi-million dollar corporations, focus on a product that has little competition and a committed group of buyers. That's exactly what a niche market is.

So how do you find a niche market or niche products? By doing a little market research online.

How to do Keyword Research

The first place to start your market research is with keyword research. Keywords are search terms and phrases that people all over the world enter into a search engine, whether to find random information or to shop for a product.

The higher the volume for a particular keyword, then (presumably) the higher the demand for that keyword.

My favorite keyword research tool is Ahrefs, which not only shows you the keyword but also all related keywords and relative competition for each keyword. It is much more comprehensive than Google Keyword Planner and easier to use, as well.

Plus, it will come in handy when you do your competitor research.

You can sign up for a 7-day trial for just $7, which is plenty of time to do all of the research that you need to start your drop-shipping business.

When you log into Ahrefs, navigate toward the 'Keywords explorer' tab on the top menu and enter your search term.

The two most important metrics to pay attention to are the search volume and the keyword difficulty. The volume, like I mentioned, is roughly how many people are searching for that particular term in a month. The keyword difficulty refers to how difficult it would be for you to rank for that keyword.

shopify keyword research - shopify keywords - ahrefs monthly search volume

Ideally, you will find a search term with a high volume and low difficulty.

While a high search volume seems like the most important metric, the magic lies within the low difficulty. The less competition there is for your search term, aka niche product, the more opportunity you have to snag all the buyers for that product.

How to do Amazon Keyword Research

Amazon is one of the most robust online marketplaces today, being the most popular place where most people purchase products compared to any other online retailer. So it makes sense that any market research that you do should naturally include Amazon.

Plus, it's likely that you'll eventually want to sell your products on Amazon, as well.

Just like you would begin your keyword research to find a profitable niche market, you will do the same within Amazon.

After all, Amazon is basically its own version of Google but with the sole purpose of selling products.

The best tool to do this research is the aptly named Keyword Tool for Amazon. It's a bit pricey so isn't totally necessary, but it will certainly give you valuable insight into the current selling trends for your particular product on the most popular selling platform online today.

Plus, you can just sign up for one month, power through your research within that month, and then cancel your subscription.

Just like with Ahrefs, you will be able to see all related search terms as well as volumes and competition score for each search term.

If you're not into the paid tool, then a free option that I love is the Chrome extension Keywords Everywhere. This extension automatically populates search volumes in the search box on a whole host of websites, Amazon and Google included.

It also has its own competition score so that you can see how many other businesses are competing for that search term.

You can pop a few of your product ideas into these tools to get an idea of both the demand and competition to make a more informed decision about which products to sell in your ecommerce store.

Social Research

Once you get an idea of the raw search terms, it's a good idea to get to know your potential customer base.

If you don't understand your potential customers and what motivates them to purchase your products, then your shop might as well exist in a vacuum.

It is important to take the time to understand

- what problem they are trying to solve by purchasing your items
- what pain points they are experiencing with your competitors
- what features they are looking for within the products
- where they gather information about which products to purchase

As you get to know precisely what motivates people to purchase items within your niche market, you can create an entire ecommerce shop that satisfies their needs.

The more that you can satisfy your customer's needs, the more likely they will come to your shop to spend their hard-earned cash.

The process of understanding the motivation behind their purchase behavior is called 'social listening.' Peek into different social media platforms to find out what people are currently saying about items within your niche and their experiences purchasing those items.

Reddit and Quora have a seemingly infinite list of community forums on virtually any topic and can provide valuable insight into the customer experience.

Facebook groups and pages are also super helpful in trying to understand what people are looking for in certain products and ecommerce shops.

Research and Evaluate Current Dropshipping Trends

eBay is still a good place to check if items sell online but don't base your prices off of eBay's. They're far too low. Even though it's not as relevant these days, it's still a good place to brainstorm profitable niches.

Once you're on eBay, you want to identify products in different niches that are expensive (to me, that's $500 or more, but it's up to you). Then go through different categories on eBay and change your search results to show "completed listings".

If the completed listing is in red it means the item did not sell. If it's in green it means the item sold.

Look closer into the products that are shown in green and search for completed listing only for that specific product. I used to do this over and over until I identified about 20 products within one niche that almost ALWAYS sold (10+ units per day).

Competitor Market Research

Even if you've found the perfect product to sell online, your ecommerce website may not stand a chance against the other websites that are currently selling similar products.

Because of this, you absolutely must take the time to understand your competitors.

Since your entire customer base will be coming to you through the internet, you will want to know how to make your website more discoverable online, whether through search engines or through paid ads. To understand this, you must understand precisely what you will be competing against online.

Basically, you need to look at the top ranking sites for your target keyword and see what kind of power these sites have behind them.

And then you need to either match that power or surpass it in order to rank higher.

So what is this power, anyway?

Well, it's made up of several things.

Search engines tend to rank websites that have a few key characteristics, including

- Relative age, or how long the website has existed
- The number of backlinks
- How relevant the content on the website is to the search term

We can't do much about how old your website is and we will tackle the content on your website a bit further in this article. The number of backlinks is what you need to focus on, now.

Backlinks are basically every search engine's form of word-of-mouth marketing. The more websites that point to your website, the more that Google sees it as a trustworthy site.

The more quality backlinks that you have, the higher your ecommerce website will rank.

The problem?

In order to beat out your competition, you will need to have as many or more backlinks than they have.

You can quickly check out a site's backlink profile in Ahrefs by going to the 'Site explorer' tab within the menu.

Fabletics is the first site listed for the search term 'yoga pants'. If I would like to sell yoga pants online, then I will need to compete with Fabletics.

I will need to compete with their yoga pants category page, in particular, which alone has 60 backlinks pointing to it.

Not only that, but the domain itself has a strong domain rating of 73, which is impossibly high.

For reference, your brand new ecommerce site will have a domain rating of zero. It will likely take years and tens of thousands of dollars to reach a domain rating of 73, making this particular search term and niche a difficult one to compete for.

As a rule of thumb, stick with a niche that has competitors with a low domain rating so that you have a chance to rank for your particular search terms.

SELECT A PROFITABLE PRODUCT

There are a couple of roads here for you to choose between. One option is to offer products in highly popular categories such as electronics, health & beauty, clothes, jewelry, etc. The obvious popularity of products in these areas means that you are participating in large markets with high demand for the products you will offer. This sounds like a desirable situation, however, it also means that the competition is intense. Again, your marketplace is gigantic and if you become a very savvy online marketer, you can do extremely well in your online business. Conversely, if you are not at or near the top of your game, you could get lost among the thousands of sites in your market.

One alternative sourcing strategy would be to offer more esoteric or "niche" products that don't have the pervasive demand, nor the fierce competition. These smaller markets may be easier for you to command and attain a high-ranking position. Additionally, smaller markets would be less price competitive and allow higher profit margins.

Consider beginning this decision-making process by turning inward and examining your own personal areas of interest or perhaps hobbies that are associated with saleable items sought by others. Your personal familiarity with a subject might make your e-business even more enjoyable.

Product Sourcing

This is one of the mission critical activities in establishing your drop shipping internet business.

Sourcing is mission critical because the choices that you make can either reward you with a smooth running profitable e-business or turn it into a customer service and/or financial nightmare.

Broadly speaking, there are lots of sources for items to be sold at retail. Saleable products are manufactured, crafted and grown. High volume items are manufactured in industrial settings in large quantities. At the other end of the spectrum, small volume items such as high quality artistic products are produced in smaller numbers and in some cases may be handmade one at a time. Organic items and food products may be grown and are sold fresh or in a preserved form.

Ways To Find Quality Products That Are In High Demand

While you're brainstorming various niches and products to sell, there are a lot of important things to consider. Here are 6 strategies to help you find a product to sell.

Accessory-heavy niches

Merchants rarely make much on big-ticket items and will only earn maybe 5 to 10% on products like laptops and TVs. Where they really make their money is on the accessories.

Accessories enjoy significant markups and customers are much less price-sensitive about them. A buyer might shop for weeks to get the best deal on a TV, but wouldn't think twice about dropping $30 on an HDMI cable from the same place. Yet there's a good chance the business made nearly as much profit on the cable as it did on the flatscreen.

When you choose a niche with lots of accessories, you'll enjoy significantly higher profit margins and fewer price-sensitive shoppers.

Low product turnover

If your product line is constantly changing year to year, you'll end up spending valuable time on resources that will soon be outdated. Selling a product line with limited turnover ensures you can invest in an information-rich website that will be viable for years.

The $100 to $200 range

I've found that this price range is an ecommerce "sweet spot." It's large enough to create decent average order value and per-order profit, but small enough that—with a quality, informative website—

most customers won't need to personally speak with someone before the sale.

As you grow, being able to generate most of your orders online offers massive efficiency savings versus a phone-heavy approach. But if you're selling products that cost $500 or more, many customers will want personal customer service before pulling out their credit cards.

Consumable or disposable products

Repeat customers are essential to any business, and it's significantly easier to sell to existing customers who trust you than to new prospects. If your product needs to be re-ordered on a regular basis—and you're able to keep your customers happy—you'll be on your way to building a profitable business with recurring revenue.

Finding a great product is only part of the equation. Even a niche fitting all the above criteria would be a poor choice in the face of inadequate demand or crushing competition. Understanding a product's demand, competition and suppliers will be important to making an informed decision.

Hard to find locally

If you needed garden equipment, you'd likely head down to your local Home Depot or Lowe's. But where would you go to buy surveillance equipment or magicians' accessories? Probably online. Pick niche products that are hard to find locally, and you'll be able to get in front of the vast majority of your customers as they search online.

While you ideally want something difficult to source locally, you also need to ensure there's ample demand for the product! This can be a fine line to walk, and we'll return to the issue in the competition section below.

Customers with a passion or problem

It's amazing how much money passionate hobbyists will spend. Mountain bikers will drop hundreds on lightweight accessories to shave a few pounds, and avid fishermen will invest tens of thousands of dollars in boats and related accessories.

Also, if you can offer a product-based solution to a painful problem, you'll find a captive audience eager to buy.

FINDING A DROPSHIPPING SUPPLIER

There are several ways to find a wholesaler or manufacturer that dropships:

Once you settle on a niche you want to target with a specific product, it is time to find a supplier that sells that product. This shouldn't be hard as there are many different dropship suppliers that offer millions of different products.

Your dropship supplier is a key partner in your business. To help you find the right one, we recommend prioritizing the following criteria:

Product samples

A major occupational hazard with dropshipping is suppliers that sell products of low quality. Before contracting with any supplier, you should request and receive samples of the products you wish to sell.

Referrals

A good supplier will provide you with referrals to other businesses they work with upon request. If they refuse, consider it a red flag.

Now that you know what to look for in a supplier, let's talk about the two types of suppliers you can work with: dropship marketplaces and manufacturers.

Fees

With margins being so low, you want a dropshipper that won't hit you with unreasonable fees. SalesHoo says you shouldn't pay more than $5 per item for stocking, packaging, and shipping. Some dropshippers will also charge you a small monthly fee for working with them.

Fast shipping (keeps customers happy)

If your supplier takes more than 24 hours to ship an item (48 at most), then they will not be a good fit for you. Dropshipping is an overly competitive market—there is no room for a lengthy shipping process. The competition will beat you if yours is too long.

On the flip side, if you can find suppliers who ship very quickly, you'll gain a competitive edge. To find the best dropshipping companies, I recommend placing a test order before you make your final choice.

No huge per-order fees

Most dropshippers charge a "per-order" fee. This is a fee you have to pay every time you place an order with them. It makes sense because they have to take the extra time and resources to pack and ship your order for you.

However, sometimes wholesalers take advantage of this and charge outrageous fees. They could range anywhere from $2 to $10. Whether or not this is high depends on the profit margins you're making on your products.

My advice is to do the math and see whether you can still make a good profit when dealing with a high fee. If not, keep looking.

Invested in technology

The latest tech in automation, efficiency, and scalability are going to be increasingly important to you as your dropshipping business grows. While not important right out of the gates, you'll want to try picking suppliers with the endgame in mind.

Some signs that a dropshipper is invested in technology include:

- A detailed website with full product descriptions
- An inventory data feed to automatically update your product listings
- The options to place and cancel orders on their website and via email

Of course, not all dropshipping companies are going to have these advanced features. Don't count one out just because they don't have a beautiful website—just keep these things in mind during your search.

Quality product (lower returns)

As we talked about earlier in the section on finding a product to dropship, finding the best dropshippers means finding the dropshippers selling the best products.

Selling a high-quality product means:

- Higher customer satisfaction
- More word-of-mouth referrals
- Fewer returns
- Better product reviews

I can't even think of any downside to selling a quality product, other than perhaps lower margins. However, the benefits above will mean more profit for your business over time than you would ever get from selling the high-margin but low-quality product.

Experienced and helpful sales reps

One thing I personally look for in a dropshipping supplier is an awesome sales rep. I want to know that I can call them and get my questions answered as fully as possible, and that they'll know how to handle any issues I have.

Don't get me wrong; no one is perfect and there will be questions they can't answer right away. But they should be willing to find the answers for you and get back to you in a timely manner.

Brand-name products

In the section on finding a product to dropship, I talked about how selling brand-name products is probably a bad idea. This is true for beginners.

However, as you advance as a drop shipping business owner, this may be a category you want to tackle. If you think you'll eventually want to sell name-brand products, this is a factor to consider when choosing a supplier.

How to find great dropshipping suppliers (that are reliable and legitimate)

Now you know what to look for, but how do you actually find great dropshipping suppliers? Are there any step-by-step methods to follow?

In fact, there are! Here are the best ways to find reliable and legitimate dropshipping suppliers:

Google

Of course, whenever the need for finding information arises, the first source we go to is usually Google.

Google is a fast way to find wholesale dropshipping companies, but it also comes with its own risks and downfalls.

The easiest way to find wholesale dropshippers on Google is by searching "[Product] + dropshipper."

Phew—1.6 million results. What's worse? You have no idea how trustworthy any of these sources are. You'll have to put each one of them through a strict vetting process

This takes time and comes with a lot of inherent risk. I definitely wouldn't recommend using Google to find your dropshipping suppliers. Why? Because the key to making great money as an eCommerce business is buying products low and selling them high.

The best suppliers are busy supplying and don't have time to work on marketing or SEO, so they're likely to be buried very deep in the search results. In fact, that's why SaleHoo was born!

SaleHoo (our directory)

SaleHoo was created by a couple of eCommerce store owners who were fed up with the difficulty of finding great suppliers, and the ease of falling into a scam.

We're a supplier directory site, and we thoroughly investigate every supplier before adding them to our categorized list. The benefits of that include:

- Lower risk—you're not going to be scammed by our suppliers
- Easier searches—filter search results based on the exact specs you need
- Faster research—quickly find suppliers' product offerings and contact information
- And more!

If you're ready to find great drop shipping suppliers who are reliable, legitimate, and affordable, learn how SaleHoo can help you now.

Alternatively, you can also check out our fully categorized list of 60 dropshippers.

How to contact a drop shipping supplier

Once you've built a small list of potential drop shipping wholesalers or manufacturers, it's time to reach out to them to see if they'll be a good fit.

Email them first. It's much easier to get the information you need via email than phone. An email will get you all the information you require without time wasted sitting on the phone waiting.

Not sure what to ask in the email? SaleHoo members get a list of free email templates to ensure you come across as professional and get all the info you need. The supplier contact emails will also save you time and increase the likelihood a supplier will respond to you.

Follow up with a call. After you send the email, increase your chances of a response (and learn more about how good a supplier's support reps are) by sending them a follow-up phone call.

What To Say To The Dropshipper

As you're thinking about emailing a supplier or getting them on the phone, you're probably wondering what the heck to even say to them, right? Here are my recommendations:

Be prepared with a list of questions. The key to steeling your nerves and sounding like a professional is being prepared. Questions help you learn more about your supplier, see if they're a good fit, and show you've done your homework.

Here are questions to ask:

What are the payment terms? Are they negotiable?

This is a pretty basic question. It will help you see their true pricing (the price listed on their website is often higher than what they actually charge) and get the best deal.

What kind of warranty or guarantee does the product have?

In order to offer your customers a great return policy for malfunctioning products, you need to know what kind of warranties your supplier gives you.

Can your service representatives answer my product questions?

While not 100% necessary, it's good to know how heavily you can rely on your supplier to answer your questions about the product. The more complicated the product, the more important this becomes.

Do you sell direct?

It's not uncommon for suppliers to sell directly to consumers in addition to selling dropshipping services. You should know this before you choose them because if the answer is yes, you are competing directly with your supplier—which could make things difficult.

What is your return policy?

Sometimes customers make mistakes and order the wrong item, and sometimes suppliers accidentally ship the wrong item. It's going to happen—you want to know how your supplier will handle this situation.

What is my expected gross margin?

Gross margin is business speak for the amount of money you make after you sell something minus the item's cost to you (also called the gross profit margin). Even if you set your own prices, your supplier should be able to tell you what other sellers are making, on average.

Do you have a data feed?

Remember when I mentioned data feeds in the "invested in technology" section? It's good to know if your supplier supports data feeds so you can easily update your store without manually entering information like quantity, descriptions, images, etc.

Are there any costs besides the direct cost of the product?

Some suppliers charge delivery fees, fuel surcharges, restocking fees for returns, or duties on imported goods. It's good to know what you're getting into ahead of time.

When might prices change?

It's not uncommon for a supplier to spring a price change on you out of nowhere. A major shift like this can be detrimental to your business, so it's important to know when this might happen ahead of time.

Can you manufacture custom items?

Part of being a store owner in the long haul is improving upon existing products to give yourself a competitive edge. If you ever plan on creating your own unique products, you'll need a supplier or manufacturer who can customize your items.

BEST DROP SHIPPING SUPPLIERS

Becoming a successful drop shipper requires some initial effort. You will need to directly contact different manufacturers to discuss the partnership details.

When you drop ship, you should pursue these two different avenues for selling your items:

- Create your own online storefront
- Advertise your listing on e-commerce sites like Wish

The more places you list, the more audiences you reach. For example, think about your own group of friends and how many people exclusively shop on either Amazon or eBay. Drop shipping suppliers usually let you sell their products on multiple online marketplaces but some platforms make the listing and ordering process seamless.

Shopify

Shopify is probably the darling of drop shipping sellers because they are in "all-in-one" drop shipping platform. You can use Shopify for the following activities:

- Partner with drop shipping suppliers
- Create an online store
- List your items on e-commerce marketplaces like Amazon and eBay

You can enroll in weekly drop shipping educational webinars and you can quickly add products to your store to begin selling immediately with Shopify's Oberlo app. Oberlo lets you list up to 500 products and make 50 sales for free each month.

Tip: Learn more about Shopify with their free online training!

Another advantage of using Shopify is that you can easily track each shipment in your storefront instead of relying on the supplier to email you the shipping details that you must manually enter into the shipping service website to track. Plus, you can sell your own physical or digital items if you have some to sell too.

So far, Shopify has helped drop shipping entrepreneurs like yourself complete more than 85 million sales!

Wholesale2B

Wholesale2B offers more than one million drop ship products you can sell online. You can integrate your Wholesale2B partnerships with your store (i.e., Shopify or BigCommerce) and also directly list your items on other e-commerce platforms too.

You have many different direct export options with Wholesale2B, but you must purchase an individual subscription with each platform you want to use. For example, you need to pay $29.99 monthly for Amazon and another $29.99 for Shopify.

Alibaba

Alibaba might be the largest online marketplace for finding drop shipping suppliers. Of course, buyers can also directly buy from Alibaba too.

Because drop shipping requires you to sell manufactured items, they are most likely going to be made overseas where production costs are significantly lower. That doesn't mean you can't find U.S.-based suppliers when you don't want to wait for a sold item to cross the ocean before it can be delivered to the buyer.

Alibaba lets you look for suppliers by region or top selected suppliers to quickly find a supplier that fits your criteria. To make sure you offer the quickest shipping times for overseas suppliers, only choose suppliers that offer "ePacket delivery" for delivery times of 30 days or less. Most international suppliers now offer this shipping option to remain a competitive buyer.

Don't forget that you can use the Shopify Google Chrome extension to quickly connect with suppliers too.

BigCommerce

You can also use BigCommerce to create your own website and list your drop shipping items on other online marketplaces too. It's possible to directly connect with several drop shipping suppliers for free through BigCommerce. In other instances, you will need to do your own research to find suppliers and then list your products on your BigCommerce store.

Once you're ready to sell, BigCommerce can automatically list your products on the following online platforms:

- Amazon
- eBay
- Facebook
- Instagram
- Pinterest
- Google Shopping

You will enjoy 24/7 live agent support, shipping label discounts, and even the opportunity to have shoppers leave product reviews to entice future shoppers to make a purchase.

Tip: Dropship your own personally-designed clothing with CafePress. You upload the design and CafePress prints and ships the item directly to the buyer!

Doba

You can use Doba for their supplier directory and inventory management systems. It's possible to directly export product listings to your store and the other online marketplaces you sell on. Doba has four different plan options, but all levels have complimentary access to the following amenities:

- Curated product category lists
- Weekly deals email
- Email support
- Supplier report cards

If you want to export your product listing to Amazon and eBay, you will need to upgrade to an Advanced or Pro plan. Additional benefits of being an Advanced or Pro plan includes live chat support and the Elite Seller Report.

This monthly report shows you the top 30 products in each category. You can also access previous monthly reports to spot trends and see which products are a long-term success.

Worldwide Brands

Unlike some of the other drop shipping directories that charge a monthly or annual fee, Worldwide Brands only requires a single payment for lifetime access. You can access their directory consisting of more than 16 million products from over 8,000 suppliers.

Worldwide Brands also has an A+ rating from the Better Business Bureau! When you're dealing with supplier companies on the opposite side of the world that you may never visit in person, building a partnership through a reputable company speaks volumes.

You can filter vendors by the following traits:

- Drop Shippers
- Light Bulk Wholesalers
- Large Volume Wholesalers
- Instant Import Buys
- Liquidation Deals

If you have more upfront capital, you might decide to try your hand at wholesaling too. Just keep in mind that you may have to rent warehouse space with the supplier so only pick products with larger profit margin or high popularity rating.

SaleHoo

One way to find drop shipping suppliers is to look for products on various online marketplaces and directly contact the manufacturer. The only problem is that this strategy takes time and you might be talking to a scam supplier.

With SaleHoo, you have instant access to a directly consisting of 8,000+ pre-vetted drop shipping suppliers. You can directly contact legitimate suppliers to forge a partnership.

A more valuable reason to use SaleHoo is their Market Research Labs. A key ingredient to making a steady income from drop shipping is picking in-demand products.

Shopping trends constantly change and using SaleHoo's research helps you stay a step in front of the competition. For example, you're probably not going to make as many sales by selling cassette tapes instead of a portable Bluetooth speaker. Although you can drop ship both of these items today, you still need to stay current with the times and preferable one step ahead.

Finally, SaleHoo also offers a community forum so you can gain advice and swap experiences with others. Newbies can also use SaleHoo's educational course to learn more about dropshipping too.

SaleHoo is an extensive directory but you still need to use an ecommerce platform like Shopify or BigCommerce to effortlessy list your products online and notify the supplier when a sale is made.

CHOOSE THE BEST DROPSHIPPING PLATFORM

Choosing the right dropshipping platform plays a key role in the success of your business. You have two choices – you can either self-host a store (build a website from scratch) or set up a store on a well-established dropshipping platform or marketplace.

Before you read up on either type and choose one, here's some commonly followed advice: it's good to choose a platform type based on what you're selling. In the end, it all boils down to how much technical expertise and funds you have, and how wide your product range is.

TYPES OF DROPSHIPPING PLATFORMS

1. Selling on online marketplaces like Amazon and eBay

Dropshippers choose to sell their products on these marketplaces because they make it effortless to run a business. All you have to do is set up an account, add your products, and start selling them. Since these marketplaces have good traffic already, bringing in customers shouldn't be a problem.

It's simple and easy, but there are certain downsides to this option. For starters, you will have limited control over your business and you cannot customize it to your liking. The marketplace you choose could lack essential features like shipment tracking, fulfilment monitoring, or website integration. Or it may limit the number of products you can offer.

If you're restricted from customizing, then your branding will also take a hit. For example, if you are selling through Amazon, and customers love your products, they are more likely to tell others that they bought it from Amazon since they will be seeing the Amazon storefront instead of your store.

You will need a good pricing strategy to handle the competition. Since there are several other sellers in Amazon, you will have cut-throat competition to handle. Also, a percentage of your sale will be charged as fee by the marketplace which could be around 10-15% of the order's value.

2. Creating your own website

The best part of having your own store is the personal branding. Unlike selling on Amazon and eBay, if a customer buys from your website, they will mention your brand name or store name when they refer your products to their peers.

Having your own store also makes the competition bearable. Since you don't have similar dropshippers selling their wares on the same platform, you can sell your products at better prices.

One limitation of having your own store is the amount of time and effort you have to invest in coming up with marketing strategies to bring in traffic to your website. You'll need to create robust marketing plans and focus on SEO to help your website to rank highly in the search engine results.

Self-hosted platforms

If you prioritize customization over anything else, and you have a sizeable budget and good technical expertise, then self-hosted platforms are a good choice. If you're building your own website, then you need to buy a domain name and hire designers and developers to create a store. This option is chosen by dropshippers who are in it for the long haul and treat their business seriously (no more "just a side hustle").

You will have to spend on setting up your website which you will be hosting in your own servers. Though you would spend a sizeable amount on setting up your site, your profit margin would be higher since you wouldn't have to pay a monthly amount or a part of the amount you've made from a sale as it is in the case of hosted platforms.

Down the lane, you will be manually setting up plugins and other integrations with self-hosted platforms. As for technical support, you can get help from online forums and support threads where like-minded dropshippers all over the world participate to help one another.

Hosted platforms

Hosted platforms are a good choice if you don't have much technical expertise, but you're willing to shell out money to set up your site. The platform is hosted by the providers in their servers and you would have to choose from one of their pricing plans. If you're going to use platforms like Shopify and BigCommerce, you wouldn't have to do everything from scratch. You can use their designs, themes and templates to customise your store.

If you're stuck somewhere or need help, you will be provided excellent customer support via multiple channels like e-mail, chats, and calls.

The only downside to hosted platforms is that customisation is limited though they provide many plug-ins that are either pre-installed or can be installed on purchase.

Which one do I choose?

Take a look at your business objectives. If you want to set up a store with a few clicks and just sell products, then hosted platforms should be fine. However, if you want to own a website completely, write blogs, get customer reviews, and fully dive into dropshipping, try self-hosting your store. Just remember that you'll have to do everything from scratch, including coding, designing, and buying a domain name.

FACTORS TO EVALUATE WHEN CHOOSING A DROPSHIPPING PLATFORM

Here are some factors you should evaluate before choosing a dropshipping platform:

Ease of setting up a store

Dropshipping platforms usually walk you through the setting up process and assist you in every step. Check whether your dropshipping platform manages all the back-end processes and allows you to choose and add your domain name.

Ease of use for customers

Your website should be customer-friendly. That means a nice homepage, neatly categorized products, and your shipping and refund policies in the footer. Choose a platform that makes all of that possible.

Consider this – an ad shows up on your Instagram feed and the product is something you've been searching for. So you click on the ad, and you find yourself on a website that looks all fancy, but the products are not categorised. It looks like a clump of random products and after scrolling for 10 minutes, you finally find the product that showed up on your Instagram feed. Whew! We're sure you've also seen websites where the homepage was a put-off and you didn't really feel like probing much after one look at the homepage.

To avoid this, you can check out the websites of other dropshippers from your niche to get an idea of what a good website should look like, and then check whether the dropshipping platforms in your list offer the customizations and features you'll need to set up a similar website.

Managing multiple suppliers

A dropshipping best practice is to have multiple suppliers or a back-up supplier to avoid out-of-stock scenarios. If you have multiple suppliers, then you need a platform that supports multi-vendor management. This involves factors like ensuring unique SKUs for products, ensuring the availability of the products, adding products from your suppliers' sites to your store with a few clicks, and so on. Your dropshipping platform should be able to help you manage multiple vendors efficiently with a streamlined order fulfilment process.

Integrations and plugins

Your dropshipping platform should be compatible with integrations and have installed or pre-installed plugins. For multi-channel selling, you need integration with different sales channels to sell across marketplaces (like Amazon and eBay) and social media channels like Facebook, Instagram, and Pinterest. You will also need email integration and payment gateway integrations to run your business smoothly.

Dropshipping plugins are useful for tasks like importing products from your supplier's list, checking your website's analytics, and keeping track of the carts abandoned by your customers.

Handling payments

Your dropshipping platform should help with tracking customer payments and notify you when your recipients have paid you. Most dropshipping platforms provide these details on the dashboard to make matters easier for the business owner.

The platform should be compatible with payment gateway integrations, and you should be able to provide a variety of payment options to your customers such as card payments and bank transfers via ACH or SEPA. If you have an international customer base, choose payment gateways that can handle multiple currencies and currency conversion.

TOP ECOMMERCE PLATFORMS FOR DROPSHIPPING BUSINESSES?

1. WooCommerce

If what you expect for your store is just very basic functionality and ease of use, WooCommerce might be an ideal solution.

Compared to Magento, WooCommerce has fewer advanced ecommerce features; in return for that, it is more user-friendly for the beginners. However, from the developers' point of view, this platform is difficult to customize and most of its functionalities must be acquired by third-party plugins.

Setup time and cost: Actually, WooCommerce is just a free plugin of WordPress framework. Therefore, you will need to develop a WordPress website first and then install the WooCommerce plugin on your store. In general, it will take less time to build a WooCommerce (WordPress) website than a Magento one if you were a developer. Therefore, if you are a non-technical user, you might still need the help of website programmers. Besides, a WooCommerce website cost is often in the range of $1,500-3,500; but if you require a lot of advanced features, you will have to spend significantly more for the plugins and customization

Ecommerce features - Your WooCommerce website will be equipped with basic and fundamental ecommerce features such as product, catalog and inventory management, pre-installed payment gateways, geolocation support, auto taxes, and shipping calculation, multiple shipping methods, discount and coupon codes, sales report, and so on. If you want to upgrade your site, there are more than 75,000 WooCommerce plugins for you to select from.

Ease of use - Thanks to the simple, intuitive and clean user interface, WooCommerce is pretty easy to use even for the newbies. Moreover, WooCommerce user guide (WooCommerce Docs) is very comprehensive, which is a valuable source for the store owners to manage their site effectively.

Scalability - It seems that WooCommerce is more suitable for small dropshipping businesses. If you are running a medium to large ecommerce store, let's go with Magento. When the number of products on your WooCommerce site increase, its performance will be affected negatively.

Support - When there is a problem, you can find the solutions by searching on Woo documentation or contacting Woo support.

Similar to Magento, to integrate dropshipping function to a WooCommerce website, you will need to install a third-party plugin (starting from $49).

2. BigCommerce

The last suggestion in the list of ecommerce platforms for dropshipping is BigCommerce. Up to now, there are over 50,000 ecommerce websites running on BigCommerce worldwide. Like Shopify, BigCommerce provides several monthly options, ranging from $29.95 to $249.95 with acceptable transaction fees.

bigcommerce dropshipping

Setup time and cost: As we have mentioned, BigCommerce offers three packages (Standard, Plus, and Pro). Also, it provides an enterprise version with undisclosed price so you must contact the BigCommerce team to know their custom pricing. Besides, it is quick and easy to set up a BigCommerce website. What you need to register an account, select a template and start customizing your store. There are 15 days for trial, after that, you must buy a specific package.

Ecommerce Features: BigCommerce provides all necessary ecommerce features for you to start with, such as order and inventory management, products and catalogs creation, supported multiple payment gateways, marketing features, integrated with ShipperHQ and ShipStation for shipping, and Avalara for tax automation, etc.

Ease of Use: For most of the hosted ecommerce solutions including BigCommerce, it is not complex for the newbies to use. After selecting a proper theme, you can easily customize it as you want without strong technical knowledge.

Scalability: Owing to different monthly plans, there is no difficult for you to scale up your fast-growing businesses when choosing BigCommerce ecommerce platforms for dropshipping.

Support: Both Shopify and BigCommerce ecommerce platforms for dropshipping provide support via email, live chat, phone, and forum. Another way for you to seek support is finding the solutions yourself with BigCommerce Resource Center.

3. Shopify

The third name on the list of best ecommerce platforms for dropshipping is Shopify. Up to now, Shopify has empowered nearly 600,000 ecommerce stores around the world, included dropshipping businesses. Especially, Oberlo, a dropshipping plugin works exclusively on Shopify, will help you to find products to sell from Oberlo Verified suppliers, Oberlo suppliers, or AliExpress suppliers.

Setup time and cost: Different from the second above ecommerce platforms for dropshipping, you have to pay Shopify a monthly fee to use the platform, which ranges from $29 to $299 per month. Besides, you might have to buy the theme for the website. Although there are 100 Shopfiy themes for you to select, only 10 of them are free. Apart from it, it's worth noting that Shopify will charge you a certain amount per sale if you integrate an external payment gateway instead of Shopify Payments. Regards time for setting up the website, this is a big advantage of Shopify. It will take only a few hours or days to create a new Shopify store.

Ecommerce Features: Overall, Shopify provides quite a lot of useful features for dropship ecommerce stores, from theme settings, products, orders and customers management, payment with credit card, multiple taxes, languages and currencies, unlimited hosting, search engine optimization, and so on. In the previous blog post, we made a comprehensive comparison between.

Ease of Use: If you are technically unsavvy, Shopify might be a good option. It does not take a lot of time for you to get used to this platform. To create the website, you just need to sign up, select a package, choose a favorite theme and start customizing it.

Scalability: Shopify is a scalable platform, you can easily scale up or down your business by choosing an advanced package.

Support: Shopify offers multiple support channels – via email, phone, live chat, forum. However, some users complained that the live chat was actually just an automatic robot system that can't help to solve our issues but gathering our email address so Shopify team can send a response later.

4. Magento

Needless to say, Magento has become one of the most powerful ecommerce platforms for dropshipping up to now. There are two versions (Magento 1 and Magento 2 – highly recommended) and two editions (Magento Open Source – free and Magento Commerce – premium) for the owner to choose from.

magento dropshipping

Setup time and cost: As we have mentioned, there are two Magento editions but the free (open source) one is enough for starting a dropshipping business. However, it requires strong technical knowledge to develop a Magento dropshipping website so that you might need to hire Magento developers. And obviously, it costs. In general, you will have to invest from $3,000-5,000 and spend 1-3 months for Magento website development. Contact us to get a detailed quote for your Magento dropshipping web development project.

Ecommerce features: It's true to say that Magento provides everything a dropshipping business needs, and even more. By default, a Magento website has fast page load speed, easy and smooth checkout, nice product and catalog page, SEO and marketing tools, comprehensive site management, and high security.

Ease of use: On the front-end, Magento websites are very user-friendly. On the contrary, on the back-end, it might be quite complicated for the admins who are just beginners without technical knowledge. However, after a short time experiencing Magento websites and thanks to detailed Magento user guides, the store owners can monitor their sites effectively and professionally.

Scalability: Magento is the most scalable ecommerce platform for dropshipping among top five. It not only enables you to create a great website from scratch with a small number of products but also supports you when your business grows. You can add an unlimited number of products, catalogs and handle a boundless number of orders.

Support: Since Magento is a widely-used ecommerce platform, there is no difficulty to seek assistance either from Magento officials, Magento community (forum), or even Youtubers who post Magento tutorials on Youtube channel. Apart from it, if you can't find help from those sources, let's think about hiring a trusted Magento agency to provide you with support packages.

In order to integrate dropshipping functionalities into a Magento website, you will need to install a third-party extension ($0-950).

5. OpenCart

OpenCart is a free ecommerce platform for dropshipping that you should take into consideration. Magento and OpenCart also share many similarities – free, open source, powerful, and more appropriate for tech savvies than the beginners. However, since Magento community is larger and far more robust than that of OpenCart, and there are more themes and extensions for Magento, OpenCart is less popular.

Setup time and cost: OpenCart is open source and free to acquire. Furthermore, you will get lifetime free support and free software updates when selecting OpenCart as your dropshipping ecommerce platform. Therefore, the major cost comes from hiring website developers and designers to build your store. Besides, it will take from 2-5 months for your website developments.

Ecommerce Features: Here are OpenCart highlights in terms of ecommerce functionalities – unlimited products and categories, multi-currency support, integrated payment gateways, various shipping methods, coupon creation for marketing, available backup and restore tools, detailed sales report, and so on.

Ease of Use: OpenCart is preferred for whom have a certain level of website development experience and website setup. However, it does not mean that OpenCart is hard for the beginner to learn how to use the platform, thanks to the user-friendly and clean interface.

Scalability: This is not a plus of OpenCart. This platform is definitely more suitable for small to medium e-commerce businesses.

Support: To get support from OpenCart, you can get in touch with them by creating a ticket or sending an email to the support team. Moreover, you can join OpenCart forum to ask other members for help.

There are several OpenCart dropshipping extensions on the market, starting from $99.

BUILDING A SUCCESSFUL E-COMMERCE BUSINESS

One excellent e-commerce marketing strategy is to create Internet Retail Stores that serve niche markets. Build your website around a particular theme and sell items that are associated with that theme. This is a strategy that can greatly enhance your probability of success in online drop shipping by including the overall theme of your site in your marketing rather than only focusing on your items for sale. Your website becomes your product! An e-commerce business constructed in this way will stand-out among the behemoths like Amazon, Walmart and others.

In the end, it will be your decision to pursue an e-commerce business opportunity. Remember, whether your website is a store selling hard goods or some other kind of online enterprise, it is not just a website. First and foremost, it is a Business and should be constructed to address fundamental reality of the way people use the Web.

BUILD A BLOG THAT IS OPTIMIZED FOR SEARCH ENGINES

Even if you have selected the perfect niche product and found the best suppliers in the world to deliver your products, it will all be in vain if you don't have customers to buy them.

So the next step is to build a site that your customers can easily find.

In a virtual world with more than 1.94 billion websites on the internet, this can be a daunting task to complete as a budding entrepreneur.

Don't stress, though. With some basic search engine optimization, you can make your e-commerce shop more discoverable to your potential customers.

You've probably seen all the buzz about search engine optimization, aka SEO, for top ranking sites and for good reason.

It is the only way to get your website seen by the eager eyes (and wallets) that you want to sell your products to.

While there is an infinite list of SEO tools and tactics to rank your website, you don't really need to use them all.

Plus, they are super time-consuming and often times expensive.

All you need is a basic understanding and a few chunks of optimized content to get the ball rolling.

Understand Search Engine Optimization

People use search engines to begin basically anything they do online.

And if you want to make sure that people stumble upon your online store in the process, then you need to optimize your website in a way that makes that more likely to happen.

This is basically what search engine optimization is.

Search engines recommend pages based on the user search query and an increasingly complex algorithm that analyzes the query a little bit like a seasoned therapist.

What I mean is, the search engine algorithm is good. Damn good.

It not only knows what a general search query means but also the thought process behind the person entering the search query.

Then, search engine crawlers scrape the entire internet in search for websites that can best answer that query.

This is where your fully optimized online store will be waiting.

In general, search engines will deem a website useful to the search queries based on specific keywords related to the queries as well as how many other sites link to it, kinda like a virtual recommendation.

As for the keywords, you've already done quite a bit of keyword research when you selected your niche product, so you should already have an idea of what to include on your website.

There are three main places where you can optimize content on your site and that is what you should focus on as you set up your ecommerce shop.

Homepage Content

Any and all text on your homepage is an opportunity to tell Google (and other search engines) what your website is about. So use it wisely.

But, to be honest, the internet is too large and too cluttered for the search engine crawlers to read every single word on every single website. Instead, they focus on the page title, the meta description, and the subheaders within the content.

While it might be tempting to put something cheeky in your title tag or headers, it is best to include one of the top keywords that you are targeting for your shop.

When the crawlers see your target keyword in the title tag, then it will know precisely what your page is about within a matter of seconds.

And that is a very good thing.

Not only that, but the title tag is also what will show up in the search engine results pages (SERPs).

As potential buyers are scrolling through the SERPs, they are most likely to click on the titles that most closely match what they are looking for, not the cute yet vague phrase that you spent hours thinking up.

Category Pages

Any of the pages that hold a category of products is, aptly named, a category page. Many shop owners lump their products onto the page and then let the shoppers scroll through them on their own.

But there is tremendous content opportunity on each of these pages that you should for sure be taking advantage of.

Why?

The search engine crawlers are extremely thorough and will be checking your category pages for clues as to what those pages are about, as well. And then they will recommend these pages to the users searching for your target keywords.

So you want to leave relevant keywords there for the crawlers to find.

It doesn't need to be all that complicated or even comprehensive. Famous Footwear does exactly this at the bottom of their category pages.

CREATE AN ECOMMERCE MARKETING STRATEGY

Once you have your e-commerce site up and running, it's time to actively seek out your customers with a solid ecommerce marketing strategy.

Because as much as we'd like to believe that all that optimization you just did will do the trick, it takes a bit of time to build momentum.

There are thousands of ways to do this, with some of these ways costing thousands of dollars, but there are only three surefire ways to grow traffic and boost sales on a low budget.

You can grow your marketing strategy later, when you're generating major profit and ready for expansion. For now, these three tactics will do.

Ways to sell, advertise, and market your products

Marketing your ecommerce store successfully may also mean you need to get to know tools like Google Adwords and Facebook Ads.

Without traffic to your page, how are you going to make any sales? It would be like writing a brilliant novel but not putting it in any bookshops.

Getting a beginner's knowledge of tools like Facebook and Google Ads, and developing your Search Engine Optimization skills, which all drive eyeballs to your site, takes a little legwork but is very doable.

Facebook Ads for Dropshipping

Facebook is the world's largest social media platform. It's a great place to advertise your products as you can tap into a huge audience. This is how Facebook makes its money, so every customer you acquire through this method comes at a cost. Facebook ads are a good option for the following reasons:

- It's easy to get started
- You control how much you spend each day
- You can target highly-specific demographics (location, interests, relationship status etc)
- It can yield fast results

- It helps to increase brand awareness
- A good ad or boosted post can go viral

For a comprehensive guide to Facebook ads for beginners, check out this post.

Google Ads for eCommerce

Google is the world's most popular search engine by far. If you have an online store, you want it to rank on the first page of Google. You can achieve this organically, or you can buy ads for your store to appear at the top of the page for the keywords you want to rank for. Google ads are a good option for the following reasons:

- You can achieve great exposure in search results
- It's the largest advertising platform in the world (Google search, Youtube, Gmail)
- You can target highly-specific demographics (location, language, device etc)
- Maximise exposure to your ads with high volume keywords related to your niche

Email Marketing

Email marketing is the unsung hero of digital marketing where a lot of the magic happens. Sure, it takes a lot of planning and even more creativity, but when done right, it is worth its weight in (digital) gold.

With an estimated $44 earned for every dollar spent, it is by far the best marketing tactic with the highest return on investment (ROI)…

…if done well.

An email blast to anyone that ever gives you their email is not likely to give you as big of an ROI as, say, a carefully structured email sequence that is tailored to your audience. The process of tailoring your emails to your audience is called email segmentation and can increase your email revenue by 760 percent.

So, yeah. A carefully organized email marketing campaign is definitely worth your effort.

So how do you tailor your email sequence to your audience?

Any good email service provider, such as MailChimp or ActiveCampaign, will have a segmentation option within their platform. They will have you install code on your website to track user behavior and then organize that data in a meaningful way.

Then, all you have to do is create the email sequence and let it run automatically.

Social Media Influencer Marketing

Influencer marketing has become a huge part of customer acquisition for retail brands in recent years. It can be particularly effective if you are in a trendy niche. For instance, if you're selling a new style of handbag, you could reach out to an Instagram model and ask if she will share a post of her with the bag, tagging your business. One post can result in a bunch of new fans and customers. The cost of influencer marketing depends on how famous the influencer is. A post from Kim Kardashian might cost $250,000, while a post from a model with 10,000 followers might only cost a few hundred dollars.

Blog or Forum Marketing

This involves finding blogs or forums that are related to your product/niche and actively participating in discussions. By positioning yourself as an authority in your niche and including a link to your website, you can increase traffic and acquire new customers.

Content Marketing

Content marketing is basically the idea of using all of the content on both on your website and website within your niche to bring in fresh organic traffic. This is under the same family as search engine optimization, making all of the groundwork you did in building your website especially helpful.

Content marketing is generally broken down into two areas

- On-page content – all of the content on your website, where you will include keywords to help communicate with search engines what your website is about
- Off-page content – all of the content not on your website that links back to your website, indicating to search engines that your site is trustworthy and reliable

If you've already optimized your website like I recommended earlier, then your on-page content marketing is sorted for now.

As for off-page content, it is helpful to create an ongoing backlinking strategy that can help you earn links to your shop continuously. The more relevant links from within your niche that you get, the more likely that your shop will rank for your target keywords.

You can view the backlinks to their category page through Ahrefs by clicking on the 'Backlinks' button on the left-hand menu.

From there, you can view the websites that currently link to their category page.

This not only gives you an idea of where backlinks can potentially come from, but also about how many you'd have to get in order to compete with a brand like Fabletics.

Social Media Marketing

When I say social media marketing, I do not mean that you need to have thousands of followers and trendy content.

Those things certainly help, but they aren't necessary for marketing.

Instead, focus on understanding your target audience and gathering data about your existing audience so that you can place super effective ads.

First, install Facebook pixel on your site to begin gathering data about the users who visit your site.

As creepy as it sounds, it's pretty essential that you do this. It will show you where your audience is based, what their online behavior is, and how they interact with your site. It will also help Facebook place your ads on pages they are visiting that are related to your page.

Basically, it does all the dirty work for you. All you have to do is create the content for the ads.

Rather than just blasting out links to your product pages and a one-liner about the product, take the time to look into what kinds of adverts work well. Look for high converting ad content ideas, in particular.

Then test it out.

Run a few tests on which ads perform better and then once you find one that works for you, double your budget on it and let it run.

TAX ID AND TAXES

After you have decided on the dropshipping business model for your new online store, you now have to form a legal dropshipping business.

Forming a legal dropshipping business obviously depends on which country you will be starting the business. We have outlined some key considerations for U.S. based dropship businesses, however for other countries see this guide here.

Here are a few key next steps to get started with a dropshipping business as a U.S. based reseller:

- Determine your business structure (i.e. Sole Proprietorship vs LLC vs Corporation etc). It is outside the scope of this guide, but here is one of the better guides we have found to choosing your legal business structure.
- Get an EIN number from the IRS and/or request a sales tax ID or reseller certificate

from your state's tax department website (see how below). It takes seconds to fill out the form. It is a quick and simple process and is required by most dropship suppliers in order to resell their products.
- Find a trusted and verified wholesale dropship supplier and open a reseller account with them. We cover this in Chapter 4: How to Find (and get approved with) Dropship Suppliers.

If you are outside the U.S., contact the supplier with your basic location details to see what documents or account details you might need to provide. In the Inventory Source Dropship Supplier Directory, we have added several filters to help find a supplier who will approve sellers from your business's location.

Getting a Tax ID for Your Dropship Business

In order to do business with real wholesale distributors, you will need to provide a sales tax ID number with your application.

To be clear, this is one of the most crucial steps in starting your dropship business. You will want to make sure to register your business legally and gain the proper certifications to do business with your supplier partners. There are many websites who will let you sell their products without needing to create this business tax ID, and it will be tempting. You might say – "That sounds great....I will go with them because I just want to sell products, not fill out forms."

You will want to avoid these programs if you are committed to building a sustainable and real business. You will have poor pricing, fees and shipping costs that will make it tough to run the business. In short, working with a company that does not require a tax ID typically need to charge you as if you are an end consumer, which means you are just buying from a retailer at retail and trying to sell to someone else with an even higher markup.

Now, a tax ID is called different things in different states in the U.S., but the purpose is the same. REAL wholesale suppliers are not charging you, the dropship reseller, any tax on the products they send to your customer. At the end of the year, they have to show the IRS why they did not charge you that tax. Your business sales tax ID number proves that you are collecting sales tax on your customers' purchases for orders shipped to an address in the state where you are based (but check with your state for their current tax rules). Your store or marketplace can automatically be set to calculate and track this tax rate. The wholesale supplier keeps a copy of your business sales tax ID number on file, so that they are not liable for the tax on the products shipped to your customers.

In the U.S., each state has a website listing information about the tax rules in that state and where you can obtain your business sales tax ID number. If you are from a country different from the supplier you want to use, there might be some additional requirements to complete your application or they might have rules preventing applications from outside their home country.

You can easily find these links with a quick google search of "How to get a Tax ID for ____ " on your own, but to make it even easier, we have compiled a list of the current details for each state. You can click on your state below to go to that site and get the information you need. Again, getting the ID will be one of the most important steps as you begin your new dropship business.

RIGHT PRICING: PRICING STRATEGY TO STAY TWO STEPS AHEAD OF YOUR COMPETITORS

Dropshipping is an e-commerce trend that offers huge profits with fewer efforts. While It seems so easy, it may not have positive outcomes always if you don't determine your dropshipping pricing policy efficiently.

Dropshipping pricing policies need to be determined perfectly.

The only source of revenue earned by you in dropshipping is the difference in the prices set by the supplier and the pricing rules modified and set by you. That difference means a lot to you. After all, it is what goes into your pocket. Therefore, you really need to be careful when it comes to dropshipping pricing.

You need to follow certain guidelines while determining the dropshipping prices in order to stay two-steps ahead of the competition.

Zero or negligible shipping costs

Always try to go for the products with no shipping cost as that would be preferred by your customers as well. You can mark your product at the cost price as you feel suitable. Shipping costs always tend to reduce the profit margin so what's the use of doing so much for a little revenue?

This infographic also says that customers would buy more if they are provided with free shipping.

Explore- It's necessary

Sticking to the same old stuff may not benefit you in the long run. Diversification, exploration is must in terms of your product line. Once your customers start liking the products on your web store, they would surely visit it regularly.

However, make sure that you provide them a good variety. Keeping the old would not always be helpful. Once you make your customers happy with the quality of your products, they would be ready to pay even more later.

Handling your returns

Profits are always welcomed happily. But, getting products returned.

That is really depressing for a supplier or a dropshipper. But, you know managing your returns well can be a blessing in disguise, just try to help out your customers. Strange, isn't it?

You need to make your customers happy. Don't get stressed. Focus on the solution rather than the problem. If your customers are happy, they are going to be regular in their dealings with you and pay you good prices. Thus, it determines your dropshipping pricing.

Avoid cheap products on your web store

Going after cheap products may not render huge returns. You need to maintain particular standards for yourself and your dropshipping store if you wish to excel in the long run. Pricing your products at cheap costs may make your customers feel that your web store offers low-quality products.

Further, the customers may not buy anything from your store. Don't form a conception that low prices always attract customers. Because it may not prove beneficial when it comes to dropshipping pricing.

Appealing products

There may be millions of customers who can't resist the products that appeal to them. You must add the most trendy and easily acceptable products to your web store and your customers would surely be ready to pay you good enough provided you have good quality products and the prices are suitable enough to the appeal and quality of your products.

Best customer services

An online store offers less expensive products but provides very poor customer services and your store offers the same products at a little higher price but with excellent customer services. You always pay heed to the needs, demands, and complaints of your customers.

Won't that make a difference? A great one, I would say.

Your customers would be ready to pay a bit more if they can trust you regarding your services and if they are sure enough that you might not run away leaving them in some sort of problem.

Discount..Deals..Offers!

Who doesn't like or get tempted to discounts, special offers, sales etc?

The best strategy is to keep your prices high in the beginning and once you feel that you are no more a first-time entrepreneur and you have started running a really great business, you can offer coupons, discounts and some special deals to your customers.

Thus, varying your prices a bit may attract a great population to your online store and can prove to be a great dropshipping pricing technique.

Flexibility-A must

Changes are always good to have. It's necessary to 'change your products', 'change your prices' and 'change your strategies'. Your business should be flexible enough.

Assess your approach to pricing often. Sometimes, you may need to make adjustments more frequently when it comes to certain marketplaces. Always keep a keen eye on your closest competitors to stay ahead of them at all times.

Strike the psychological aspect

It is a common psychology of your customers that they would prefer the products ending with odd numbers. Mark the price of your product as $7.99 and your customers would round it off as $7 and not $8. It's a bit strange but that is a common observation.

PRODUCT DESCRIPTIONS

Your product descriptions are your last ditch effort to convince Google to rank your products and customers to buy your products.

This is where you list both the product features and benefits, two key points that people search for when they begin the buying process…

…and two key points that convert them from shoppers into buyers.

NastyGal does a great job of not only fitting in key features of their products, many of which users will be including in their search queries, but also making them sound fun.

Automating the Drop Ship Process to Increase Profits

Automating an online drop ship program using e-commerce software can turn even low margins and small dollar items into real profits. Full end-to-end automation of the various drop shipping functions should include the following items.

- Formal purchase orders (POs) go out to suppliers in real time as orders come in.
- Suppliers provide shipping information, actual shipping cost and tracking numbers back to the retailer as orders are fulfilled.
- Customers receive automatic shipping notices.
- Suppliers are prompted for status on aging orders.
- Amount owed to each supplier for the pay period is automatically calculated.

Using e-commerce software that automates the drop shipping process makes the program easy for the retailer to manage as without automation, the customer service and order management staff must be much larger. A retailer can spend money on automation once or can spend it on people ongoing. Software is much easier to manage than people as there is no hiring and firing, no vacations, sick days or medical plan to manage. Using automated e-commerce software for drop shipping will maximize the retailer's profits.

E-commerce software with drop ship automation also makes it easy on suppliers. Suppliers get a list of open orders; a running account of amounts owed and payments made plus reports on how much of what item the retailer is selling for them. Automation makes the entire process paperless and transparent.

Once a product in the shopping cart is linked to a supplier, the purchase orders for that product can go out automatically. Any technical questions can go to the supplier just as easily.

Additional Considerations for the Retailer

Suppliers should want to drop ship for your store. Why should a supplier drop ship for you? Combining various suppliers' product lines produces synergy in any retail business plus you can carry their complete line. In a stocking model, a retailer must choose which products will sell the best. With a drop ship model, the retailer can carry all of a supplier's products without concern for inventory turns. In the case of a manufacturer, you will also be promoting their brand name which is very important to smaller or newer companies.

You have choices with credit card processing. Should you authorize and capture immediately or authorize only and capture after shipment? For items that are shipped within 48 hours, authorize and capture can be a fully automated process using drop shipping software.

As with many business decisions, the choice to run a drop ship program does have its pitfalls and risks. Credit card fraud, returns, damaged goods, and backorders are all more complicated than running your own warehouse as each supplier will have its own policies.

Backorders can be minimized by integrating your shopping cart with your supplier's inventory availability software. This helps avoid both backorders and order cancellations based on lack of inventory. Your e-commerce provider can provide this integration for you as an extra service.

$10,000/MONTH STRATEGIES: DROPSHIPPING SECRETS TO SUCCESS

A lot of us would want to start our own business. The only thing that is stopping is the investment that we need to fund a business venture. There is an answer to do that you can start a drop shipping business online.

With drop shipping you do not need to have a huge investment to start one. Here are some tips to have a drop shipping business that you can be proud of.

Pay Attention To Design

The design of your site doesn't have to be award-winning, but it does have to look polished and professional.

When you're designing your store, you'll want to ask yourself: What do you want your visitors to feel when they browse your site?

The answer to this question will vary with your target customers and the products that you're offering them.

For example, if you're selling home exercise equipment targeted to a female demographic, you'll want them to feel inspired, motivated, and confident.

The next thing you need to ensure is that the information on your site is complete, organized, and accessible. For example, make sure all the policies they need to know are published in full, clearly organized into sections, and easy to find on the page.

In addition, don't deviate too much from the familiar. For example, your customers would expect a navigation menu bar at the top of the page and links to your privacy policy and terms and conditions down on your footer bar. Don't change around these elements too much that your customers become disoriented.

Different designers will probably have different ideas on the perfect layout and the perfect colors. But the most basic thing you need to remember is that the optimal design of an ecommerce site is one that doesn't take attention away from the products and helps customers make purchases smoothly and painlessly.

The Power Of Demonstration

Demonstration in dropshipping terms is marketing your product in use. This a key to understand psychological persuasion tricks for dropshipping. Instead of having pictures of your bracelet on a table, have pictures of a girl wearing it on an actual wrist. This will increase conversions for sure. Why? Because customers like to imagine themselves wearing it. It's much easier to do this when you provide pictures of people using your product.

It doesn't have to be clothing either. If you're selling a lawnmower accessory, provide pictures of it in use. It is better if the people in the pictures are similar to your customers. If you are advertising a hat for college men, make sure your model is a college man. This helps with provoking an emotion in your potential customer.

Provide Stellar Customer Service

Standing out from the crowd is important, especially if you're selling in a high-competition niche.

One of the best ways to stand out is by providing outstanding customer service.

And I don't just mean replying to their questions and comments, or honoring your return policy. Those are bare minimum customer service requirements that you should be doing.

I'm talking about truly going the extra mile for your customers to make their experience with your store memorable.

Convincing happy, loyal customers to repeatedly purchase from your store is much preferable (and easier) than convincing more and more prospects to buy from your store.

Here are some ideas to make your customer service really exceptional.

Talk to your customers. I mean, really talk to them. It can be time-consuming and tedious, but knowing what they need and expect from your store will make it worth your while.

Set up an automated email for customers who have bought from your online store to ask how they're finding the product, what other products they'd like to see in your store, and whether the purchase went smoothly.

Invite them to reply to that email and assure them they'll get a personal reply or even a phone call from you. Keep this promise! Get in touch with everyone who does reply so you can get a deeper insight and have an actual conversation with your customers.

Don't expect everyone to reply, but show your gratitude to the ones who do by giving them an incentive, like a free gift or discount codes.

Most importantly, take note of the feedback that they've given. Bring them up in your store newsletter and set up a poll to know if other customers share the same sentiments.

Treasure your customers. Treat your customers right and they'll buy from you again. Think of unique ways to make your customers feel appreciated.

You can send personalized thank you emails after they purchase something from your site. Basic courtesy goes a long way in getting them to remember your online store.

Add discount codes for customers who have purchased a certain amount on your store. For example, you can give 5% off discount codes to customers who've purchased a minimum of $50. Experiment with not advertising these codes and just giving them out as surprise gifts.

Another way you can express your heartfelt gratitude is by holding monthly giveaways through electronic raffles exclusively for those who've purchased from your site.

Consider starting a loyalty program. Probably everyone is familiar with basic store loyalty programs. Buy something from a store, get points for your purchase, then exchange your points for rewards, normally free items from the store.

The good thing about having an online store is that you can award points for actions other than purchases. You can award points to your customers for doing actions as simple as registering for an account or liking your Facebook page.

There are many more steps you can take to provide the best customer service possible. Remember to do as much as you can to make your customers feel valued and appreciated. Your customers might not always remember what they bought from you, but they'll always remember how you treated them.

Use Scarcity/Urgency

Scarcity is when you state there is a limited number or products remaining. For example, " Only 20 necklaces remaining, hurry!" Urgency is when you state there is a deadline for the sale. For example, "Only 24 hours left of the Christmas sale, buy now!" Both can work tremendously well to increase conversions. Be careful if you're using both though as this can often be overkill.

Dropshipping is all about forcing the impulse buy. You do not know the customer you are trying to target on Facebook. They are simply scrolling along and happen to stop and click on your ad. We are selling low ticket items (less than $100), which means customers will make up their mind on the spot whether they will buy or not. Yes, you can do retargeting (and we'll be talking about this in a future article) but it's the impulse buy we're chasing for the most part.

Focus On Marketing

It's easy to get overwhelmed with other details that are less important.

Marketing brings in the customers who'll buy the products that you're offering in your store. Without customers, you'll have no profit. No marketing, no customers.

Here are some aspects of marketing that you need to work on.

Content marketing. Your blog might be a little neglected at this point because of all your activities with your dropshipping site. But getting visitors to your blog can also draw traffic to your store.

Creating unique content on a regular schedule is a great way to build an audience and educate your visitors about your products while keeping your website updated. Don't constrain yourself to creating traditional blog posts. You can also create videos and photo galleries to showcase your products.

SEO. Don't neglect your search engine optimization (SEO) efforts, either. You want to be found by your visitors through search. More content means more keywords you can optimize for, increasing the chances that you'll be found.

Social media. Remain active in your social media platforms. You can always automate a percentage of your posts, or repost old content or other peoples' content (with attribution!) so that maintaining your online reputation doesn't eat in too much of your time with other activities for your dropshipping store.

However, your social media accounts should be active when curious visitors look at them. Replying to comments, engaging with your audience, and building a strong rapport with your followers should be part of your daily routine.

Create Irresistible Offers

Once visitors are on your site, do everything you possibly can to motivate them to buy. Presenting the right product with the right offer might just be the push they need to make that purchase.

Here are some offers you can experiment with on your site.

Bundle deals. This is an ages-old technique done by merchants to get people to buy slow-moving merchandise: bundle them with your best sellers for a reduced price.

When you're dropshipping, though, you're not keeping inventory, so doing bundle deals isn't really a matter of "getting rid of slow stock." Your objective is to increase the amount that your customers spend per transaction.

For example, instead of spending $10 for a novelty phone case, offer a novelty phone case and a basic phone case for $15 that would cost $20 if ordered separately.

Upsells and cross-sells. When your customer is going through checkout, it can be assumed that they already have their credit card out, ready to buy whatever they placed in their cart.

Upselling a product that is similar to what they're purchasing but an upgrade (e.g., more features, more premium look, rare color) as they're checking out might just push them to spend more on that order than they would have. If it doesn't work, at least they now know that such a product exists.

A cross-sell might work at checkout as well. You might already be displaying related products to your customers on the product detail page, but showing these related products to customers as they're checking out already checking out could convince them to add those items, especially if you reduce the price.

Bulk discounts. For instance: "Buy 4, get 1 free!"

You're trying to get your customers to buy more of a product, so make it more attractive to them. Again, the point is to get them to spend more on a single transaction, so make it worth their while to buy more of a single item. This normally works for less expensive items.

Flash sales. One of the simplest ways you can use urgency to increase sales is to add a flash sale page or section to your store, where you can add particular products that are on sale for a limited time only.

You can do it by product category. For example, if you're selling makeup, you can have makeup brushes on sale Monday, then lipsticks Tuesday, then eyeshadows Wednesday, and so on.

The urgency is emphasized if you have that countdown timer ticking down the minutes/days before the sale is over. It's also generally better to display it prominently on your navigation menu so that visitors know there's a flash sale going on.

Discount codes. Online shoppers are mostly bargain hunters as well. Discount codes can help push your visitors or casual browsers to finally try purchasing from your store.

You can offer discount codes to customers who reach a certain purchase amount. For example, you can give customers who've spent $100 discount codes for 10% off on their next purchase. This helps secure repeat customers.

Social media discount codes are also being used by many online sellers to attract their social media followers to their stores and convince them to buy. This also helps them track which of their social media platforms are attracting more customers.

You can also place discount codes on group buying sites like Groupon or LivingSocial. This will give your site exposure to a greater audience, even though this audience is comprised of deal hunters.

Emailing exclusive discount codes to your mailing list is a good way to persuade your blog subscribers to transition from readers to customers. Plus, that exclusivity is a good way to retain loyalty.

Use Benefits Over Features

Features are listing traits of the product. For example "Our mug is red and holds 300ml of liquid". Benefits are the positive outcomes the customer receives. For example "Our mug is red to bring you Christmas cheer during holiday season. It holds 300ml of water to allow you to enjoy a large cup of relaxing tea to make your holiday season perfect". Do you see the difference there? Benefits always win out over features.

The reality is human beings do not care about your product. They care what your product can do for them. That's why you must change the default Aliexpress product descriptions. They simply list the features without stating the benefits to the customer. The art of writing words that sell is known as copywriting. Amazon does a better job than this compared to Aliexpress if your interested to learn more.

Keep An Eye On Your Competition.

Plenty of other entrepreneurs have discovered dropshipping and how it can be a profitable online venture. And chances are you aren't the only dropshipper who's targeting your chosen niche.

Competition isn't necessarily a bad thing. There's a good deal of knowledge to be learned from your competition, especially the biggest ones. Take advantage of this knowledge and apply it to managing your own store.

At the risk of sounding like a stalker, I'd recommend checking their online store, following them on social media, and even possibly subscribing to their mailing list.

Take note of what products they're selling, how they're describing them, the quality of their blog and social media content, and how they talk to their mailing list subscribers. Take note as well of which products they seem to be talking about more than others, and which channels they tend to share these products on.

A word of caution, though. Garnering this much information about your competition doesn't mean you should copy everything they do. Respect their intellectual property: don't plagiarize their content, don't steal their product photos, and don't copy their website design. If you get caught, you might get your business closed down, or worse, be heavily fined.

Sell What You Know; Know What You Sell.

It pays to sell products or at least product types that you already have knowledge in. If you know what you're looking for in a product, you'll know what your target customers are looking for as well. This gives you a major advantage when researching products, because you're more likely to choose products that your audience will love.

Choosing products you already know also makes it easier for you to write descriptions that play up a product's best features and take product photos to feature details that are important to you and your customers.

It's not enough for you to sell what you know, though. You also have to know what you sell; that is, you have to continue using the products that you sell, reading up on them, being updated to changes in how they're manufactured, and researching competing products or alternatives.

Knowing what you sell makes it easier for you to answer your customers' questions about the products that you're selling and recommend bundle or package deals based on which of your products go together.

Know about your products more than the average buyer.

Start Small

When you're starting out, it's tempting to add as many products as you can to your store.

You might feel in the beginning that the more products you offer, the more respectable your store looks like and the more likely customers will buy from you.

While that may be true, you're creating a ton of work for yourself at the very start. For instance, if you add 100 products to your store, that means you'll have to create 100 quality product descriptions, find or take 100 sets of product photos, compute optimal prices for 100 products, and, well, you get the picture.

By starting small, you can focus on writing higher quality product descriptions, taking higher quality product photos, and optimizing prices and discounts in a smaller amount of time. Once your store takes off and you get some sales, you can then add more products every month.

For instance, you can start with just 20 products, sell them for 4 weeks, and when they're profitable, you can add 10 more products the following month. This can go on until you reach an optimal number of products, whether it's 100 or more.

While you're at it, don't hesitate to remove products that are giving you problems, such as negative reviews or shipping delays, or are just not earning you money. Sometimes cutting down the fat can help your store become even more profitable.

Learn To Recover Abandoned Carts

Shopping cart abandonment is when customers add items to their carts without actually completing the purchase. You've probably done it once or twice, both in physical stores or in online stores.

As a consumer, we know that abandoned carts are normal, but as an online store owner, abandoned carts suck because there's no way you can find out what your customer was thinking at that moment before they closed their browser, or whether in fact it was them who closed the browser (your site may have crashed, their connection may have been interrupted, etc.)

There can be lots of reasons why customers abandon carts. They may have been surprised with the shipping costs, or they may not like being forced to create an account on your site, or they find the checkout process too tedious.

The good news is that you can still do something to try to save the sale. There are now apps available to automatically email customers who have left items in their cart (provided they've provided their emails at that point).

Not all dropshippers know how to do this, so it's in your best interest to study how to do this at the start.

Study Product Photography

When you import products from your suppliers into your store, they normally provide you with product photos you can use on your site without watermarks or any other identifying marks that they came from other sources.

While getting ready-made photos is certainly convenient, it's going to benefit your business more if you learn how to do your own product photography. Suppliers may work with plenty of other dropshippers, not just you, and might be providing the same product photos to everyone who carries that product in their store.

Taking your own product photos works to your advantage first and foremost because it proves that you have the product, you've used it, and you can vouch for its quality.

This is especially important to show customers who've been eyeing the product and may have seen other sites carrying the same product. Your original photos are surely going to stand out from other sites who have the same photos from suppliers.

An additional advantage is that you can take photos of the products you're selling when they're in use or when worn. It helps customers visualize themselves using your product when you show the product in context.

One more advantage of taking your own photos is that they're yours. You can place your own watermark and protect it as intellectual property.

The most important equipment you'll need is a decent DSLR camera. It doesn't have to be top-of-the-line, but it does have to take amazing, high-resolution photos. From there, there are lots of courses available you can take to hone your photography skills.

If you already have a knack for photography, then don't be afraid to experiment and snap away. Always keep in mind what your customers will be looking for in your product photos.

For example, if you're selling clothes, you'll want to have photos of every color and style available, and you'll want to show how they look like when worn. By contrast, if you're selling an electronic gadget with plenty of features, it's more important to show closer views that really show the details.

Commit To A Consistent Schedule

Following a regular schedule lets customers learn what to expect. Consistency makes you appear more professional and serious about your business.

Plan in advance when to post content on your blog, newsletters, and social media. Upload new products on the same day or days every week. Schedule your flash sales with the same product categories on a particular day of the week.

Publishing on a schedule encourages your longtime customers to know when to check back for your new blog posts or new product offerings or flash sales on products they love.

Find your Goldilocks schedule (i.e., not too often, not too rarely) and stick to it.

Request Product Reviews (And Publish Them).

Providing social proof that other customers have purchased your product (and loved it!) can help increase your sales.

When you start getting sales, include a request for a product review on your post-sales email series (after thanking them for their purchase). You can even encourage them to post photos of the product on the product page.

As your sales (and customer base) increase, look into automating product reviews. There are applications for Shopify and WooCommerce that enable you to automatically ask your customers to leave reviews for products they've received.

Here are some more things you should keep in mind when dealing with product reviews.

Respond to both the negative and positive reviews. Negative reviews are a part of the eCommerce hustle. It's how you deal with them that can make or break your business.

The fact that they took the time to leave that review means that they probably want to give you the chance to redeem yourself. Reply to those negative reviews with steps you're willing to take to turn a negative experience into a positive one.

For example, if they're unhappy with the product quality, offer a refund. If they received a damaged package, offer to send a new one. Owning up to your mistakes can turn an unsatisfied customer into a loyal one.

However, don't neglect your positive reviews. Online store owners usually only respond to negative reviews. While this is obviously good practice, you don't want to ignore customers who have positive things to say. Take the time to reply to them and express your appreciation for their kind words.

Take action. Reviews are only valuable to your business when you pay attention and act on them.

One-off problems with orders can be considered normal, but constant problems with product quality or deliveries should be addressed. It might be time to change suppliers or take the product off your store.

Prepare Yourself And Your Business For Turning Points.

Dropshipping, like any other business, can present plenty of challenges and obstacles. When you encounter turning points in your business, you'll have to be ready to change your course or even abandon ship if necessary.

The speed at which change can happen is even more accelerated for an online business. To keep yourself and your business afloat during turbulent times, you must develop a mindset that's ready to handle turning points and make the necessary changes.

Examples of turning points in your dropshipping business can include your supplier suddenly becoming unresponsive or failing to ship products to your customers, or a new trend in your niche that you want to capitalize on.

Your competitors can unexpectedly drop their prices, or one of your blog posts can unpredictably become viral, increasing traffic such that your site crashes or increasing orders such that your suppliers can't handle it.

Turning points, good or bad, force you to implement some changes on your online store and your business in general. Know this from the start and brace yourself so that you remain level-headed and not make rash decisions that can destroy your business.

An In Demand Product To Sell

In drop shipping you do not need to have lots of products to sell. Just research what product is currently on demand. You can not just sell anything you want. You need to look for a product that a lot of customers would want to buy or needs.

Hottest Trends

To keep abreast with your competition, be sure to check out what is the in style at the present. Do not let your site be outdated. Customers would tend t wander to other websites for their shopping needs if you can not supply them with what they need.

Keep on Educating Yourself

Having a business means constant education. The world is changing fast and to be ahead of what is the newest technique in marketing you have to continuously do your research. Having the right marketing technique can reward you with great profits in no time at all.

With these in mind your drop shipping business would surely be successful. In no time at all, you will be enjoying the financial freedom that you have been dreaming of.

Customer Friendly Websites

It is important to have a website that your customers will find easy to use and navigate. Be sure to make your website attractive to your customers to make them come back for more and even refer some of their friends to check out your site.

HOW TO START DROPSHIPPING WITH SHOPIFY

How to Start a Successful Shopify Dropshipping Store

If you are wondering how to start a dropshipping business? Here are the 10 steps to create and run a successful Shopify dropshipping business.

Step 1: Identify a profitable niche

Finding the right niche for your Shopify eCommerce store

You cannot pick products to sell at random in the hopes of turning over a profit. To maximize the performance of your drop shipping store, you need to identify the niche for your shop before you create it.

By researching the best possible products to sell based on various factors, you can highly increase the chances of making a sale and turn your initial efforts into passive income for years to come!

When it comes to unearthing the best niche for your Shopify dropshipping store, here are some of the recommended practices:

Sell products that cost between $1-20

When selling using the dropshipping method, you need to consider overhead costs when taking orders and placing them with your third party supplier. By targeting products at this price range you can also maximize earnings by marking up prices as much as 60% over wholesale rates. An additional benefit is that the capital involved will be more minimal.

Target upper-middle-class customers

You want to appease an audience that not only has purchasing power, but also disposable income. The middle class with an average annual income of between $41,000 and $132,000 is your ideal target market. They will be more than willing and able to spend on a product that they need and want.

Sell products with no discernible brands

It will be harder to penetrate a market with predominant brands hawking sales. To make the most out of your store, you need to sell products which have fewer or no popular brands dominating the market. Doing so allows you to have a fighting chance to make money from your shop.

Free eCommerce tools to determine your niche

The factors mentioned above are just a basic overview of the things you need to consider when choosing a product niche

At this point, you want to justify your choice by researching keyword difficulty and performing a competitor analysis. Below are additional eCommerce tools that you can use to validate the niche you want to sell in.

Google Keyword Planner

Google is the search engine that people use. For sites that rank on top of search results for their respective keywords, they are getting not only lots of traffic but also likely conversions. Therefore, you can leverage the keyword data (using Google Keyword Planner) to determine a profitable niche.

Google Keyword Planner for business use

Front page of Google Adwords Keyword Planner.

For the purpose of niche product research, this tool will help you find keyword ideas that you ought to potentially sell on and ultimately rank for your shop.

Upon logging in; you will gain access to a general overview of the keyword's search volume. As a site owner, you want to find keywords that are frequently searched for online. These keywords can help increase your chances of getting found by your customers, assuming that you do rank for your chosen keywords.

You will need a Google account to use the tool. To use the Keyword Planner, click on the "Sign into Adwords" on the homepage.

After logging in, click on the "Search for new keywords using a phrase, website or category."

Search for ideas for your eCommerce store

Login > Search for new keywords using a phrase, website or category.

Next, enter a product that you're interested in selling.

As an example, let's assume that I want to find watches to sell on my store. Therefore, I can type "wrist watches" on the product or service bar. You can narrow down your search by identifying the product category and the location of the search.

Scrolling down the list of keyword ideas will show you different keywords relevant to your initial search. Through the results of my search, I decided on pursuing the "wrist watch for men" keyword.

SEM Rush

While the Keyword Planner is good enough to provide you with keyword suggestions to target, it does not show how difficult it is to rank for them.

Keyword difficulty is determined by the quality of sites ranking in the first ten positions on search results for the keyword. The quality can be drilled down to different on- and off-page SEO factors. Trying to untangle all this data, regardless of your experience with SEO, will eat away a chunk of your time, which is something that you can't afford.

What you need is a separate tool that will help you figure out the keyword difficulties. One great tool that can help with this is SEM Rush.

While SEM Rush is a paid tool, you can still use it to extract the keyword difficulty of a limited number of keywords.

Upon creating an account and signing in, enter the keyword in the search bar and click on the "Search" button to show the data.

Once the page loads, scroll down the Phrase Match keyword section and click on "View full report."

On the report page, scroll down the bottom to show the related keywords and their different metrics.

What you want to focus on is the keyword difficulty row. The lower the Keyword Density (KD), the easier it is to rank for that keyword on search engines. Currently, the keywords are arranged from the most difficult to the least.

Also, "wrist watch for men" has a KD of 90.71 and takes the top spot for the most difficult keyword to rank for. What we can do is search for another keyword that we can consider optimizing for our Shopify store.

To arrange them from the easiest to the most difficult, click on the KD letters.

Use SEM Rush to determine the keyword for your eCommerce store

From the results, you will see that the keyword "antique wrist watches for men" has a keyword difficulty of 67.03, which means that it's easier to rank for this keyword in search results.

By choosing this keyword, we will also have to narrow down our selection of wristwatches to dropship those with antique designs. Putting these data to real life –

Spocket

Spocket and Orbelo are shopify dropshipping apps you can use to look for dropshipper. Use Spocket or Orbelo dropshipping apps to search for products to dropship

Ali Express

Ali Express is the place to look for dropshipper. Use Ali Express to search for products to dropship

While most of the watches shown in AliExpress (screenshot #2) are pocket watches, there are wrist watches available in the result. Also, considering that the keyword we want to optimize for is not very difficult to rank for ("antique wrist watches for men"), the product is ideal for sales on our Shopify store.

It is important to point out that the keyword has a search volume of 20 on SEM Rush. While volume is crucial, our goal is to rank on top of search results with our store. Therefore, we need to choose a keyword that's relatively easier to rank for. Choosing keywords with high volumes and a KD of at least 85 will take you more time and effort to rank for the keyword.

Ideally, you want to select keywords with low keyword difficulty scores.

Step 2: Choose A Supplier For Your Dropshipping Store

Using the information above, you should be able to find the best possible supplier. When it comes to finding a supplier who will provide you with the items that you will dropship on Shopify store, you can't go wrong with

AliExpress.

using aliexpress Shopify dropshipping apps to source products and look for dropshipper

Using AliExpress for dropshipping business is easy and convenient. Shopify recommends AliExpress as your primary source for all your dropshipping needs and offers this guide to help you get started.

If you don't have a product to sell, you can use the search bar to brainstorm for ideas.

Typing in "dropshipping" will reveal lots of results you can choose from.

For the purpose of this example, let's click on "dropshipping watches" and see the products we can choose to dropship on Shopify store.

Here's the search result we got.

Judging from the results, the products being sold cost between $1-20, which meets the criteria for the best practice of dropshipping. Potentially, this is something that you can sell on your Shopify store.

Now that you have the results hover your mouse cursor over any of the items. You will see metrics that you can use to filter your suppliers from the page.

using aliexpress to look for dropshipper and source products for your dropshipping store

Below the price, you will see the star rating from the feedback of its customers. To its right, you will see the number of users who rated the supplier, as well as the number of orders for this particular item. From here, you need to consider the product's star rating and the number of people who rated it. The higher the star rating, the more reliable the product/seller is.

If possible, try to find products which have been rated highly by many users. If only a handful of people gave a product a perfect score, then you may want to find another product with a comparable score that is rated by hundreds of users.

When choosing products to sell in your Shopify shop, go with non-branded ones. Since it's difficult to tell from the naked eye which products are genuine which ones are knockoffs, it's best to avoid them altogether. Go with generic products that have high ratings on AliExpress to sell on your online shop.

Below the product rating is the supplier rating as represented in diamonds. Even if the product is top-notch, another influencing factor would be how responsive and easy to deal with the supplier is. Thankfully, the diamond rating will give you a glimpse of the supplier's reputation in AliExpress. Hovering your cursor on the diamond will show a feedback summary from its customers.

Click on the diamond to show more feedback information.

As a rule of thumb, you want to reach out to suppliers with a feedback score of at least 95%, which is a good enough indicator of the supplier's reliability.

Perform these steps when looking for products and suppliers to reach out to then narrow down your choices to a couple and start reaching out. Communications with them will give you a more direct idea of how responsive they might be.

Since we're planning on targeting wrist watches for men, let's look into other available wristwatches on AliExpress.

The price point of this watch is perfect ($7.99) – it's not too expensive, and you can mark up the price for a reasonable amount.

Based on the quality (4.7 out of 5) and volume (87 users) of reviews, as well as the volume of orders (94), it is safe to say that there's good potential for the product to sell well because the supplier has received high ratings from its customers.

To compare and scale the price that we want to sell the wristwatch at, let's go to Amazon and find similar items to the one we're planning to sell.

From the screenshot above, the price of leather wrist watches ranges from $20-$200. For this purpose, let's set the price of the watch to $20 to remain competitive.

At this point, it is best that you order a product sample from the supplier to see how convenient it is to purchase from him or her. Assuming that you chose a supplier with a high feedback score, you shouldn't have any problem ordering the product to your doorstep. While you can just rely on the ratings shown on AliExpress, ordering from them will give you better insights on what customers can expect once they order from the supplier through your shop.

For now, we need to message the supplier for clear product images and the description of the products that you can feature on your Shopify store.

Finding product supplier for my shopify dropshipping store - chat history

Based on the conversation above, you can secure details within 24-48 hours. This is a good indication that the supplier is responsiveness and shouldn't be a problem to deal with regarding product details or other issues. Perform these steps again for other products you're interested in selling on your Shopify store.

Step 3: Signup And Choose A Shopify Plan

Now that we have a niche and product in mind it's time to set up our eCommerce store.

To begin, click here to create your Shopify account. Signing up is free, just input your email address, password, and the name of your shop.'

Signup for your shopify store

Upon successfully signing up, Shopify will ask you questions of questions to aid in the setting up of your store

Regarding the first question, you have four choices to choose from:

- I'm not selling products just yet
- I sell with a different system
- I'm just playing around
- I'm selling just not online

Since you don't have a shop and want to create your Shopify dropshipping store, you can choose "I'm not selling products just yet" in the meantime.

For the question, "How much revenue does your business currently make in a year," you can enter "$0 (I'm just getting started)."

Once you've chosen those answers, click "Next."

You will then need to complete your order details by filling out your personal information.

After submitting your details, you will be redirected to your dashboard.

Shopify Plans

Once you have created your account, you need to subscribe to a plan to unlock all of Shopify's premium features. While you still have a 30-day free trial, it's best to settle your plan from here on out, so you also don't have to worry about this later on. To do that, once you're in the dashboard, click on the "Select a Plan" button.

There are three plans to choose from – Basic Shopify, Shopify, and Advanced Shopify.

Since you're just starting out, it's best to choose the Basic Shopify plan. Later on, assuming that your shop takes off, you can change the plan to take advantage of more features. Compare features and pricing of Shopify plans in Jason's Shopify review.

Step 4: Setup, Design, And Configure Your Shopify Store

From here, let's set up your Shopify online store. Below are the things we need to tackle when creating your eCommerce store:

- Purchasing and setting up a domain
- Setting up email forwarding
- Choosing a theme
- Create "must-have" pages for your Shopify store

Setting up a domain name for your store

First, you need to go to your Online Store page and click on "Domain."

Using a domain for your Shopify store is optimal. However, the main reason why you should consider buying a domain is for branding purposes. Without a dedicated domain, your store's URL will be:

https://nameofshopifystore.myshopify.com.

While you don't have to pay for a domain if you don't want to, a domain name would be more beneficial to your customers. With one you can have full control of how your URL would read – likely much more user-friendly, like this:

https://nameofshopifystore.com

It will be much easier for your target market to remember and type your domain name into their browsers.

More importantly, being able to spend for your domain shows that you are serious with your online store, which gives off a better impression to potential customers.

If you ultimately decide on buying a domain, click on the "Buy new domain" button on the page; or, go with a third party, ie. Namecheap.

NameCheap costs $10.98/year for a .com domain, $14.98/year for a .net domain. The best part about NameCheap is that all domain purchases come with free WhoisGuard (used to be $15/year), which masks the identity of domain owners.

It's recommended that you register your domain name with third-party registrars – just in case you wish to move your eCommerce store in the future. For domain registration, we recommend Namecheap and GoDaddy. GoDaddy is the biggest (not one-of) domain name registrar while Namecheap is super competitive in term of pricing and customer support.

The most common domain extension, .com, costs $13 on Shopify. If you want a unique extension, you can choose from its wide selection of premium, albeit more expensive, domain extensions.

For now, let's stick with the .com extension. Click on the "Check Availability" button.

On the next page, you will find out if the domain name is available for purchasing. If so, you will be required to fill out a form to complete your order.

Before you can click on the "Buy domain" button, you need to check the box to show that you agree to the ICANN policy and DRA.

After clicking on "Buy domain," you will receive an email notification that requires you to click on the link to confirm your purchase.

Configuring emails

When running your dropshipping with Shopify, you need to realize that you work as a middleman between customers and suppliers. Usually, when someone places an order you will manually relay the order to your provider so they can process the delivery and ship to the client.

Setup email forwarding for your shopify store

To set up your email forwarding, go to the Domain page and click on your purchased domain.

On the next page, you will see that there are two emails set up under your domain: info@ and sales@. If you want to change the email address where all your emails from your Shopify store are forwarded to, then you can make the changes here. To delete the existing emails, just click on the trash icon and confirm the deletion. If you want to add a different email, (e.g. change the address to customerservice@ or support@) you can click on the "Add an email address" link here.

Enter the email name of your choosing and the email where you want to receive the messages.

Choosing a Shopify theme

It is important to put some thought on how your store is designed. A big part of the reason why is because you want to provide your visitors with a rich, seamless experience when browsing your site. If they like how your site feels, along with its content, then there's a good chance that they will order from your store.

To get there, however, you need to choose the right theme for your Shopify store.

The default theme is named as "Debut". There are dozens more free themes available at Shopify. To change the store theme, go to Themes setting in your Shopify control panel.

A new window will open to load the Shopify Themes. There are different themes and styles to choose from – some are free while some cost up to $180. If you are just starting out, it would be wise to select from the pool of free themes first.

For this example, let's choose the JumpStarttheme (the middle theme). Clicking on it will lead us to the activation page.

Before you confirm using this theme, you may want to look at its features and see if you can use them to make your Shopify store look better for your visitors.

If you are sure that you want to use this theme, click on the "Install Theme" button.

You need to click on "Publish as my store's theme" link to finalize the change in theme. If you want to install the theme but not override the current theme, click on the "install as an unpublished theme" link.

A new page will appear with a "Go to your theme manager" button that leads to your Shopify page where you can customize your theme. Click on the button to make the necessary changes in your theme.

After clicking on the "Customize your theme" button, you will be led to a page where you can edit your theme.

On this page, you will see many sections on the sidebar that allow you to edit your site. Clicking on a section will show you the different customization options to choose from.

Most of the options are pretty self-explanatory so it's best if you can play around with each to see which works best for you. If there are sections in your chosen theme that you don't have any use for, click on the tab, scroll down the bottom of the sidebar, and click the "Delete section" button.

Adding store pages

Since Shopify has no idea that you plan on building a dropshipping store, you need to create pages that will help inform your visitors about what your shop is all about. Below are some pages I highly recommend you create for your Shopify store.

- About
- Products
- Shipping
- Returns
- Contact

To begin creating your new page, go to the Pages section under the Online Store category.

Once you clicked on the "Add page" button, you will be directed to the page where you can create new pages on your shop.

The text editor is in your usual WYSIWYG (what you see is what you get) style where you can format the content based on different options to choose from. If you know how to publish content using a blogging platform or a CMS (content management system), then you'll have no problem editing content on Shopify.

Below are guidelines that you need to consider when creating pages for your

Shopify store:

About – The purpose of this page is to explain to visitors and supplier what your dropshipping store is all about. Be as comprehensive as possible and cover as much ground as you can when talking about your shop.

Products – Showcase the list of goods and collections you're selling in your store. Also, explain why people should buy from you and what makes your products better than your competitors.

Shipping – Mention how long each order (big or small) will take to be shipped out. Also, talk about delivery methods and other details that they need to know before purchasing from you so they can have an idea of what to expect.

Returns – Discuss your return policy here. Mention the maximum number of days before a customer can return the product, refund policies, and who will pay for return shipping, among other details.

Contact – There will be details that you won't be able to cover on your store pages. If so, your Contact page should open the line between you and your customers for questions, inquiries, and concerns about your store and products.

Edit About Page for your shopify store

Since you also want to attract more organic traffic from search engines, you want to edit configure your page's SEO right. Scroll down the page and click on the "Edit website SEO" link.

Edit the meta title and description with the goal of attracting more clicks from users once they see this in search results.

Once finished, click the "Save" button to finalize your page.

After creating the page, you want to include the page on the site's navigation, so visitors will easily see the page. To do this, after saving your newly created page, click on the "add it to your store's navigation" link.

You can add the page to the footer or main menu. For this example, let's include the About page on your main menu.

Add about page

Once you are on the main menu page, add the About page to the list.

Once you're done, click "Save Menu" to finalize the changes.

Do this on all of the mentioned pages that you need to create for your site.

Refund, Privacy, and TOS statements

If you want to generate quick pages for these statements, go to Setting > Checkout and look for the "Refund, Privacy, and TOS statements" section.

The statements generated by this section will appear in the footer of your checkout page. As mentioned on the side part of the page, the templates are not legal advice so you need to edit them with help from a legal expert to make them binding.

Step 5: Add Products To Your Shopify Dropshipping Store

Add products to your shopify store

It's now time to add your niche products to your store. To add a product page, click "Add product"

Full up product details

Once you are on the Products page, you need to fill out the details of your product.

For the description, you may want to edit whatever that's given to you by the supplier. Make your descriptions more compelling to convince your target market to purchase it from you.

Product details

On the right sidebar, under the Organization section, you need to edit the product type and vendor to categorize your product for the benefit of your visitors. You can also include this product in a collection so you can lump together similar products and showcase them to your potential customers altogether. Lastly, you must enter keyword tags for your product so visitors can locate it on your search bar.

Product page title and description

Below the product title and description is the Images section. Upload all the images provided to you by the supplier. Make sure that the images are hi-res and of excellent quality to improve the chances of getting people to purchase your product.

Product pricing

For the pricing, enter the most appropriate price based on your research. Comparing the watch to the ones sold on Amazon, we settled at $20. It is arguable that we can increase the price to boost our profits, but the pricing above is merely an example.

Adding product delivery details

Regarding shipping, you can also leave this blank since your supplier will manage it. However, you need to discuss the details with your suppliers on how to proceed with each order to ensure that the products get delivered on time.

Shipping

Below Shipping is the Variants page which lets you set the different variations of a product. If your products are available in different colors, sizes, and others, then you need to enter it here, so people have options to choose from and potentially increase conversions.

Finally, you can edit the product's search engine listing. Click on the "Edit website SEO" link to input your meta title and description, as well as the URL.

For the page title, you may want to consider adding your dropshipping store's name at the end if there are enough characters. For the meta description, you need to be as detailed as possible about the product. Maximize the available 160 characters as efficiently as possible so you can convince users browsing search results to click on your link. Regarding the URL, you can also edit it to shorten it if possible.

You also need to consider a keyword to optimize for this product page. You can use SEMrush to find keywords that are not difficult to rank for so you can increase your chances of ranking higher on Google or Bing.

Once you're done, save the product. Apply the same process for all of the product you plan to sell on your Shopify dropshipping store.

Automatically adding products to your collection

The benefit of creating a collection of products is to compartmentalize products with the same brands, type, theme, or other factors that bind them together.

Using the product we entered above as an example, let's say we want to sell more genuine leather bracelet watches on our shop – we would use a collection.

Create collection page

On the first half of the Create collections page, enter the name and description of the collection. Apply the same principles used for creating your product here. Be as descriptive as possible so you can provide the necessary information to visitors to help them make an informed decision.

For the Collection image, ideally, you want to upload an image that shows most of the products you're selling, so visitors will have an idea of what to see and purchase from your collection. If not, you can probably download the product with the best image regarding quality.

To make products much easier for you to add to your collection, you can automatically add newly created product pages based on certain conditions. You can choose from product type, price, vendor, tag, and others, so you don't have to enter them in your collections manually. You can also add multiple conditions to ensure that products that meet any one of the conditions you entered will be included in the list.

Finally, edit the page's SEO so you can compel more people to click on your link as it appears in search results.

Once finished, click on the "Save collections" button.

Step 6: Add A Payment Gateway To Your Store

As an eCommerce site, you want to provide the shopper with different payment methods so they can use whichever method is most convenient for them. Normally, shoppers would use PayPal or credit cards for online transactions. Regarding the latter, you can use Shopify Payments so you can accept payment directly through Shopify – no setup required.

Shopify payment for your eCommerce store

Shopify payment.

One of the best features of Shopify Payments is the ability to keep track of all transactions made via your Shopify dropshipping store. Also, if customers want a chargeback from their purchase, you can respond to them with a customized template to make your life easier as a shop owner.

Unfortunately, Shopify Payments is not available in all countries. If that's the case, thus the next best option is using PayPal for transactions.

Paypal at shopify

By default, all purchases will be made using PayPal Express Checkout. You can also accept credit cards through this payment gateways, and there are no transaction fees, so you get to keep all the profits.

Credit card payment at Shopify store

Regarding credit cards, if you want to accept payments using a third-party processor, you need to choose from the list available under the "Accept credit cards" section.

Shopify offers hundreds of payment options that will surely satisfy your target audience. With a list of options this huge, you can't make an excuse that people can't buy from you because you don't accommodate their preferred payment method.

All you need to do is choose the payment gateways that you want to set up from the list, assuming that you're already subscribed to the gateways you will be selecting. If not, you will need to sign up for them. Once you have chosen from the list, you need to fill out the necessary details to process your option so you can accept payments via credit card using your preferred gateway.

If you want to add more payment options, refer to other applicable methods under "Alternative payments" and "Manual payments."

Step 7: Configure Your Store Shipping Rates

Depending on the products you're selling, you need to edit your shipping rates so you can provide accurate pricing.

Configuring shipping rates

To configure shipping rates: Login > Settings > Zones and Rates

To calculate shipping costs accurately you need to know the following:

Shipping rates

Look at the prices of shipment depending on the size and weight of your products for local and international delivery. Pricing will often be different based on multiple factors.

Surcharge rates and volume

These are fees necessary to additional factors, such as bringing the shipment to customer's doorstep.

Supplier expenses

These are costs that you have to pay the supplier first to get the product prepared and ready for shipment.

Again, there are no universal rates for these fees – you need to talk to delivery service providers and your suppliers about their pricings. From here, you can come up with a reasonable price for each of your items that factor all the costs mentioned above.

For more shipping configuration tips, read this article at Shopify.

Additional shipping methods

Working with additional shipping methods at Shopify.

On Shopify's "Additional shipping methods" section, you can enable third-party calculated rates at checkout if you have a Shopify plan or higher. This lets you automate the process of calculating shipping costs, so you don't have to figure it out for yourself and manually enter them.

If you want to take away the hassle of arranging the shipping of products to your Shopify dropshipping store, you can add a dropshipping service to delegate all orders to your dropshipper or supplier.

Upon clicking on the page, you can connect with popular fulfillment services like Rakuten and Fulfillments by Amazon through an app from Shopify. However, since your supplier will be coming from AliExpress, you need to confirm first with your supplier if they can deliver products on your behalf.

Step 8: Add Gift Cards And Discount Codes

If people are shopping on your site for gifts but are not sure which item to buy their loved ones, then a gift card is an excellent choice. By assigning a particular amount to each card, customers can use the card for products that add up to the exact amount of the card.

You can offer your own gift cards for purchase in the same way as you sell your other products. You can also give the cards away to customers who just purchased from your store. Either way, if used right, gift cards can help increase the sales of your dropshipping store.

Gift cards

To create your card, go to Products > Cards on your sidebar menu and click on "Start selling gifts on my store."

Create gift cards at Shopify

However, to enjoy this feature on Shopify, you need to have a Shopify plan or higher.

Once you have upgraded, you will be lead to this page on the site:

Gift card configuration page

After creating the variants for your gift cards, you can save them on the "Online Store" under the Visibility area to make the cards available for sale. You can also issue the gift card to select customers to reward them for their loyalty.

Discount code

You can increase sales by getting visitors to become customers. Try using discount code so they can purchase your products at lowered prices.

Discount codes at Shopify

On the sidebar menu, go to Discounts and click on "Add Discount." Fill out the details as seen on the screen above. Make sure to edit the Conditions and Usage limits according to your intended settings so that customers won't misuse or overuse your discount code.

Once you have created your discount code, you need to promote it on your online shop so that people will use it for their transactions. Below are ways that you can do this:

- **Promote on social media** – Share the code on Facebook, Twitter, and other social media channels.
- **Write a blog post** – Publish posts on your blog section that explains in detail your discount code and how to use it. You can then share the post on social media instead of directly sharing the code there to drive more traffic to your blog.
- **Create a pop-up** – Pop-up forms are a great way to build an email list or drive traffic to a particular page on your site. The form will dynamically appear on any page on your shop to attract attention to it. For more information about pop-up forms and tools, read this Shopify post.
- **Send an email blast to subscribers** – If you want your discount codes to be used only by people who signed up to your email list, then you can send them to your list using an email marketing platform. Use discount codes as an incentive for people to sign up on your mailing list. If you don't have an email list yet, check out this post on Shopify to fuel your imagination and creativity so you can apply the ideas on your store.

While discount codes are effective in driving sales and increasing revenue from your Shopify dropshipping store, you shouldn't offer these all the times.

Indiscriminately giving away discount codes can result in fewer sales and lower customer engagement with your store.

Step 9: Setup Customer Support

Even if you try to cover all the information about your Shopify dropshipping store on your site, there will always be questions that didn't occur to you when you were building your online shop. Therefore, you need to make yourself open to customers who want more details about the products you're selling, as well as the status of their orders.

The simplest way for people to reach you is by having a contact page in your store that they can quickly fill out with their queries and concerns. However, some people would prefer a faster and more convenient way for them to reach out to you instead of waiting for hours and days for a reply.

To solve this, you need you to provide better lines of communication from your Shopify site with your customers. One of the best tools that can offer the complete package is ZenDesk.

Zendesk + Shopify

You can set up ZenDesk to cover the following aspects of your Shopify store's customer support:

- **Phone** – Through ZenDesk's Phone feature, you can give the human connection your audience yearns for when it comes to expressing their concerns. The tool also takes care of customer history. Automatic ticket creation and call recordings help agents focus on solving issues at hand instead of worrying about workflow.
- **Chat** – To provide users with quick answers to their concerns about your shop, chat support allows them to message agents for assistance. By resolving problems immediately, you can expect to increase your sales and offer a better user experience.
- **Knowledgebase** – You can create a customer portal that combines the collective knowledge of your agents based on the questions they receive from users and callers. The knowledge base will serve as a one-stop guide for all potential problems or issues your customers have come across, so they don't have to talk to or email to your agents.
- **Social media** – Some users prefer to make their voices heard through social media and messenger apps. With ZenDesk Message, you

can address their concerns right on their favorite social apps and platforms.

ZenDesk's pricing is flexible depending on the features you want to use for your Shopify store. For $5/month you can get email and social channel support, a basic help center, and a widget that will appear on your screen. This is the perfect plan if you are just starting out with your Shopify dropshipping store. If demand rises, you can shift to a different plan to accommodate more features like performance dashboards, multiple ticket forms, and more.

ZenDesk comes with a 14-day free trial for each plan so you can test it out and see if it can become your go-to platform for all customer support needs.

For more details in installing Zendesk to your Shopify store, refer to this article for the necessary steps.

If you feel that ZenDesk is too big for your needs, you can choose any of the smaller tools below:

- **Drift** – Take live chat to a whole new level! Place a floating button on all your pages that visitors can click on. They can posts questions

and comments easily, and you can reply just as quickly as well!
- ***Grasshopper*** – If you want to take calls from your customers, this tool lets you create a branded 1-800 or local number that directs to your smartphone or any of your support team.
- ***Hootsuite*** – This popular social media management tool lets you view all your social media profiles in a single place so you can answer and reply on multiple channels from a centralized command center.

By using any of the tools above, you can aim for better conversions and a happier customer base.

Step 10: Launch Your Shopify Dropshipping Store

Even as you may have been editing your store up to this point, it is still not yet available for public viewing.

launching your shopify dropshipping store

The reason for this is because your site is password-protected. It makes sense as well because you're still in the process of building your store up before you can show it to your target audience. To open for business, you need to remove password protection.

Once you have done the steps above, it's time to unlock the site and provide access to the public.

After clicking the button, you will be directed to the Password page section of the Preferences page. All you need to do here is un-check the "Enable password page" box and click on the "Save" button.

HOW TO START DROPSHIPPING WITH AMAZON

Would you like to start dropshipping on Amazon, but don't know how to do so profitably? In this article I'm going to reveal the step-by-step instructions that you need to open up your own Amazon store.

Normally on our YouTube channel, we don't recommend dropshipping on Amazon. Why? Well, it's because most people want to use Chinese dropshippers that they find on Aliexpress. Unfortunately, this is a saturated method and it doesn't work. But there is one way to dropship on Amazon… and that is with USA-based dropshippers!

- Step 1: Set up an Amazon seller account (important details you need to know, keep reading).
- Step 2: Find the best dropshipping companies that have items for low prices.
- Step 3: Go through the catalogs of these businesses and identify the lowest-cost items that have good buyer demand.
- Step 4: And finally, you need to actually list these items on Amazon in a particular way that

will get people clicking on your listing and buying your items.

Step 1: Setup an Amazon Seller Account

Before you can begin dropshipping on Amazon you're going to need to create a seller account. We strongly recommend selecting to create a professional account.

Step 2: Locate Low-Cost Dropshippers

We recommend the low-cost (but very valuable) tool, SaleHoo, to locate low-cost USA dropshippers. It is a supplier directory list containing over 8,000 low-cost, reliable suppliers. It is the secret source of cheap suppliers and dropshippers that people (like me!) are using when dropshipping on Amazon:

Basically, the gist of this step is you purchase a subscription to SaleHoo, and then use their internal filters to look for local suppliers that dropship. The reason you want local dropshippers only, is because when a buyer purchases an item on Amazon they expect it usually within 5-7 business days maximum. If you are located in the United States, and have a dropshipper located in China, then it will usually take weeks for your item to arrive at your customers doorstep, and they will be unhappy. You can sell items with longer shipping times in your own store, but not on Amazon:

When dropshipping on Amazon, you need to research local suppliers. Select "more options" to filter suppliers.

You might think that you could just find SaleHoo's suppliers for free using say, Google, but you can't. Unfortunately, most suppliers have very small marketing budgets and so they won't show up in the search results since their websites are not designed from a marketing perspective. You either need to use a paid directory like SaleHoo, or find them at trade shows.

Step 3: Go Through The Catalogs Of The Suppliers You Just Found And Identify Their Low-Cost Items

Back in step 2, you might've wondered why we were looking for low-cost dropshippers before we even knew what we wanted to sell. Shouldn't we figure out the best items to sell before we find suppliers?

Well, if you know what you'd like to sell you should do that, obviously. But if you don't know what to sell, I recommend finding the suppliers first, and then going through their catalogs and figure out the best items for dropshipping on Amazon.

Which are the best items to sell? Items that are listed well below their going price on Amazon. This means that you can list the same item on Amazon for the same price as other similar listings.

Take this one item. It was selling for $59 from the supplier…

This was one item that was selling for $59…

But on Amazon, similar items were selling for $129.99 + shipping costs:

To see what this item is, download my free ebook.

When you work out the profit margins on that, it works out to be over 109% after Amazon takes away it's fees:

When dropshipping on Amazon, look for items like this with high profit margins.

So this item was be perfect for dropshipping on Amazon. The suppliers were selling it for a price much lower than what similar items were selling for on Amazon.

Step 4: Write Amazon Titles And Listing Descriptions That Convert AND Catch The Amazon Search Engines

Once you've gone through steps 2-3 and found the low-cost suppliers and the best items in their catalogs to dropship, it is time to actually list them on Amazon. When listing them on Amazon, there are some tips and tricks you can use to outrank your competitors in the Amazon search engine and write more compelling sales copy to steal their sales:

- Long, descriptive titles that are rich in keywords rank well in Amazon. The same goes for item descriptions.
- Buyers like knowing about refunds as it makes your listing seem more credible (luckily most of SaleHoo's dropshippers have a refund policy).
- Sending out emails after each sale, asking people to please leave a review (this can increase the numbers of reviews you get by more than 10x!).

HOW TO START DROPSHIPPING WITH EBAY

Starting the eBay Dropshipping Company was one of the best things I've ever done with online work during my career. I was initially skeptical about eBay, but it was one of my most successful Internet companies ever. Ebay is great for companies that want to start making money online through a low-risk system with a good return.

The eBay market is very large and continues to grow daily. They continue to grow their customer base and sellers are increasingly making full-time revenue on the platform. If you learn how to do it correctly, you can also start eBay and earn a full-time income over the period. This isn't too difficult, but to succeed on the platform you need to know a few things.

Let me explain what eBay Dropshipping is before I get into the details of what you need to do if you want to be successful in eBay Drop Shipping. EBay Dropshipping is a business model where salespersons' list products on the eBay market without seeing, storing or touching the product. All you need is to find an item to sell from a trusted provider, list the product for profit on eBay and start selling. The business model is very simple, but it works. A simple video that explain dropshipping in eBay .

Now I'm going to take you through a few simple steps to set your benchmark on starting an eBay Dropshipping business.

Finding Your Niche

You first have to decide which type of product you are going to sell before you actually start your eBay business. Will you sell in one, two or three or different categories? Are you interested in the products you sell on request? Is it possible for you to participate in the competition for this product? As you can see, you first need to answer a number of questions. If all these questions cannot be answered right now, you may need to do some research in advance.

You can do your research in several ways, either using the eBay marketplace itself, or using tools and software designed to do so. ZIK Analytics is among the most popular. But if you can say yes to all the above questions, we can move on to step two.

Create Your eBay and PayPal accounts

You'll need an eBay account and a PayPal account to sell products on eBay. These can be installed freely and the process is very simple and easy. You will need to enter your business information such as your credit card details and your eBay and PayPal addresses. One important thing is that when you start eBay you have a certain sales limitation on your account.

- The amount of items you can sell in your first month on eBay will be limited. If you're a good seller, this will increase every month.
- You won't have immediate access to it when you sell your funds. Usually, a few days after your items have been received by a buyer, eBay releases your funds.

These are temporary limits. Ebay protects its customers against fraudulent sellers. Thus, vendors on the eBay platform need to build a reputation.

Suppliers & Sourcing

You've done your research now and you're clear about the kinds of products you're going to sell. Next, you have to figure out where those products will come from. Hundreds of providers are available to you and this is very dependent on your niche as different suppliers offer different types. Amazon, Walmart,

Target, Home Depot, Sears, Doba, Salehoo are among the most popular eBay suppliers. These are just a few examples of where you can access the products from the source when you start an eBay drinks company.

Most of the above suppliers are bigger ecommerce giant, meaning you don't need their authorization or before you've approved them to use them as suppliers. But starting to use suppliers like Doba, Salehoo and similar wholesale websites as dropshippers is a much more tedious task. You wish to contact this supplier using wholesale suppliers, negotiate and confirm minimum ?uantities, prices and payment methods. You are ready to start listing your items when all of this is finalized and agreed.

List Your Selling Products

The listing of your items for sale does not differ greatly from the organization of the brick and the mortar shop on the right shelves. This is your opportunity to impress your visitors and help persuade them to shop. The quality of your listing is a crucial factor in the amount of sales you make. The eBay list creations have four main elements and are:

- Complete title optimization
- A Quality image

- Product description in detail
- Best price in market

Complete Title Optimization

Shoppers are looking for keywords; please give great titles to your products. This determines how many visitors you are visiting. A free tool to help you build a good title called the DSM tool.

High Quality Images

Quite often the images of your supplier will be good enough to show your eBay store on their website to show them. However, in some cases, images may be too small based on the eBay specifications, so a photo editing tool may be required to increase image sizes and possibly increase brightness, etc. Please note that the pictures are your product and you want to talk about the high quality as you see a potential customer.

Product Description

Make sure you have a detailed product description written in readable format. Give no more than 250 words and no less than 200 words of information you can about the product. Use paragraphs and bullet points to make it easy to consume. Take your product description as your sales pitch and use it to share the benefits of the product you are trying to sell. This will increase your sales substantially. DSM Tool has really nice description templates.

Best Price in Market

Don't pay too much for your items. You want your products to be priced at a time when you profit after paying Paypal and eBay fees, but you don't want to be priced off the market. Look at the competition and try to align as much as possible with it. But in a price war, don't enter the competition. Fix and stick to the desired profit that you want to make on your items. Pro tip: 10 percent net profit is considered to be ideal.

Managing Your Business

As you can see, starting an eBay Dropshipping business is not that difficult. However, there are a few key things you need to know about and do if you want to make long-term money for your business. Even if you're easy to do things, you may lose your business faster than you actually started if you're not doing things right.

E-commerce markets like Amazon and eBay are brutal when it comes to sellers operating on their platforms. They have strict customer experience policies, meaning you must always offer the best customer experience. If you don't, your sales account will strike and your business will suffer a single strike.

Some of the things you need to take into account when running your eBay store is that your stock levels and price changes need to be continually updated to remove order cancelation from your seller account. To have too many cancelations is the easiest way to remove your selling privileges. But managing these adjustments manually is almost impossible. The fact that many newbies try to do this manually is the majority of the failing eBay dropshipping companies. However, all this can be solved by using a tool called Dropship Management Tool or, shortly, DSM Tool, which eliminates manual processes from your company. This tool automatically drops shipping for you up to 95 percent of your business in eBay.

Another very important thing for you to know and understand in running your eBay business is the importance of good customer service. Their feedback system is one of eBay's main customer service factors. Good service can help you boost your eBay company during and after sales in a short time. EBay also allows you buyers to receive feedback as a seller whenever you make a sale. Make sure you use the opportunity to leave your feedback because it can encourage the buyer to return a feedback. Feedback helps you build trust with buyers and definitely helps you sell more on eBay. The more positive you get, the more you promote the eBay algorithm in your store.

HOW TO PROMOTE YOUR BRAND AND YOUR PRODUCTS

When it comes to promoting a new product or service for your business, it can seem like there are endless options. It can be difficult to figure out where to get started and which methods of promotion will give you the best results. The truth is that there are many ways to promote your business, and what works may depend on your business. Here are 10 ways to promote a new service or product for your business.

Social Media Contests

Contests, giveaways, and sweepstakes are a very popular tool among top quality marketers. Why? Marketers know that social media contests work!

Social media contests are a fun, easy way of connecting with customers and bringing in more fans for your social media platforms. A simple Facebook contest for example, garners 34% new fans on average per campaign. That's huge considering that organic reach is low on Facebook!

Instagram giveaways give customers an exclusive chance to be the first person to get their hands on your new product—for free! The giveaway can be marketed all across your social media channels and through email. Run an Instagram giveaway to get more direct traffic, put your business in front of new customers, and for a fun way to connect with fans.

Post to Google My Business

You can post about your new product or service to Your Google My Busines profile in two ways. The first is to create a Google post and choose the "promotion" option. The second is to upload photos of the new product or service to your profile. For help, check out Tip for Adding Photos to Your Google My Business Profile.

Connect your Google account to see how you can easily improve your presence across four key areas of Google local search.

Host an Event

Another way to get people to your physical location is to host an event or an open house at your business. Hosting an event is a great way to get people physically into your business, which makes them more likely to become a customer. Events don't have to be fancy and super organized; something as simple as an open house or an info session will work for locations like salons, fitness centers, yoga studios, spas, and retail stores.

If your business is in a location with other local businesses, you can work together to have a sidewalk sale or outdoor open house to draw even larger crowds! This is a great way to promote a new product or service that you're offering.

Offer an Upgrade or Trade-In

If your business is more service-based than product-based, like a salon, spa, fitness center, or consulting business, you can offer an upgrade for customers to try out your new service. Offering a new facial or massage at your spa? Provide a complimentary upgrade for existing customers to try it out! Expanding your consulting services? Offer expanded services to loyal clients so they can see the difference!

If your new product is, in fact, an upgrade on an older one, you can consider crafting a trade-in promotion. Trade-in promotions are proven to be effective because they incentivize consumers to buy a new product using a token or credit they already have (the product they own). You can also resell the old trade-in products, provided they are in good enough condition, or use them for future giveaways.

Facebook Ads

With 1.44 billion monthly active users, Facebook is a window to a huge market. That's why Facebook ads are an effective marketing tool. Facebook is particularly useful in concisely targeting your audience, as Facebook's impressive data collection allows businesses to target by gender, age, location, interest, and more. You also have an array of options for the type of ad you want, and you can easily stick to your budget by creating a cap on how much you want to spend daily or monthly.

Offer Customers an Exclusive Preview

Your loyal customers are a key part of how to promote your product, because they are most likely the first ones who will buy it. Offer customers an exclusive preview of your new product. This can take the form of a private, pre-launch party, an online preview, or a special invitation to test out your latest service. These exclusive offers to loyal customers will make them feel good and keep them coming back.

Email Marketing

Did you know that 82% of consumers open emails from businesses, and that 44% of email recipients made at least one purchase last year based on a promotional email? Email marketing via newsletters is a fantastic vehicle for advertisement, and is one of the best ways to promote a new service or product.

Email newsletters allow you to easily share news of your product, photos, and information with customers. From there, offering an exclusive discount or promotion is a great way to "seal the deal" so to speak, and get cash flowing your way. For more ideas, check out this post on email newsletter topic ideas.

In-Store Promotions

Businesses with brick and mortar locations have the added opportunity to promote a new product or service in-store. If you want to know how to promote your product in your studio or store, the #1 thing you need to do is to give people a reason to go to your store.

Aside from having attractive logos and signage, you can promote your new product or service in store with signs and promotional materials inside. Offer exclusive in-store discounts, such as a buy-one-get-one-free or a percentage discount. You could also market your product as being exclusively available at your retail store. Whatever your promotion, be sure to emphasize that it won't last forever. Customers whose purchase power is limited, either by time or inventory, feel a more pressing sense of urgency to buy when it comes to your product.

Share Customer Reviews

One of the best ways to promote a new product or service is to let your customers speak for you by sharing reviews. If you take advantage of some of the ideas previously mentioned and offer an upgrade or free preview to customers, ask them to review the new service or product online or to provide a testimonial for you to share. People will be more likely to sign up or try it out if there's a glowing review from another customer.

Share on Social Media

Another way to promote new products and services is to announce and share this on social media. If you're using the tactics mentioned above, make sure to share any of them on social media, including: customer exclusive events, open houses, trade-in or upgrade opportunities, giveaways, customer reviews. and photos. If you find that customers are posting on social media sites like Facebook and Instagram, make sure to share those photos with your own followers to entice people to try out your new service or product!

HOW TO USE SEO TO SKYROCKET YOUR BUSINESS GROWTH

If you've been ignoring the important topic of SEO, get on top of it now! You're leaving clients and money on the table. Read on to discover the basic essentials that will get you on the road to effective SEO for your business

If you're a business owner, you need to get your head around the topic of SEO, or Search Engine Optimisation.

WHAT IS SEO

SEO is the practice of increasing the quantity and quality of traffic to your website through organic search results in Google and other search engines.

SEO is critical to your business because it's how people find you. If you're a remedial massage therapist working in the eastern suburbs of Melbourne, you want to make sure that if someone in eastern Melbourne searches for a remedial massage therapist, you show up in the search results!

You might have heard the saying:

The best place to hide a dead body is on page two of Google search results.

Tweet it

It's funny, and also metaphorically very accurate! If you can't find what you're looking for on page one of Google search results, you usually just refine the search and try a different search term, right? So obviously, you want to do everything in your power to rank on page one of Google search results.

Google is increasingly the go-to tool to find anything on the internet for the majority of the population, so it's important that you harness it correctly. Search traffic has grown by 2000% in the past 20 years. In 1999 Google processed one billion searches, and now that number is up to 2 trillion searches per year! The average person conducts 3-4 Google searches per day (for more mind-blowing stats on Google, check out this article 27 Mind Blowing Stats About Google).

SEO all starts with understanding the keywords and phrases (long tail keywords) that people are searching for when they're trying to find a product or service that you offer. It's all well and good to use fancy language and phrases on your website, but if people aren't actively searching for those terms you're using, you won't appear in search results.

The first step in any SEO practice is to undertake what we refer to as 'keyword research'.

There are some great free tools that are available to do keyword research such as the Keywords Everywhere browser extension, or the Keyword Tool, or the Answer the Public site. Take the time to research your keywords extensively. Spend at least 1-2 hours doing this if you can. And once you have an extensive list of commonly used keywords and long tail phrases that people are searching for in your field, you should keep them somewhere where you can access them regularly, and make sure you use them across your website.

There are two ways you can build your SEO capability – with 'on-page SEO' and 'off-page SEO'.

Have you ever wondered how to get a basic handle on SEO to make sure you're making it easy for people to find you and to get great rankings in search engines? Read on to discover the basic strategies of SEO that will get you a long way to optimising your business growth.

'On-page SEO' is all about getting those keywords into as much content on your website as possible – blog articles, page titles, picture descriptions.

You want to eventually have an even spread of keywords throughout your website, however the most important places so start with are your page titles, post titles, and meta descriptions as a minimum. If you can get your important keywords into titles and meta descriptions, you're well on your way to maximising your SEO.

Obviously you don't want to go overboard and do what's called 'keyword stuffing'. Keyword stuffing is trying to get as many keywords into your site as humanly possible. But it will ultimately work against you because it doesn't look or sound natural, and your top priority should be making your website a positive user experience so that people spend longer on your site and become returning visitors (both great qualities for increasing your rankings in Google). Plus, Google algorithms are extremely clever and they can always recognise when someone's trying to 'keyword stuff' – and it'll work against you!

Other forms of 'on-page SEO' include things like proper URL structure, user-friendly 404 pages (for when a link is broken), mobile-friendly pages and a fast loading page (I can't understate how important it is to find a fast host! I highly recommend Little Bizzy for fast-loading hosting and great customer service). Slow loading pages simply won't rank highly with search engines and your potential clients will click away before your site has had a chance to load.

'Off-page SEO' refers to the activities that are performed beyond the boundaries of the website, which include link building, social bookmarking, social media marketing, content marketing and more.

Make sure you're doing these essential things and you'll start growing your business with ease.

HOW TO HANDLE SECURITY ISSUES WITH YOUR BUSINESS

Having information about clients and customers is important, but ensuring that private information remains secure might be just as vital to the health of a business.

Here are some suggestions for securing your systems and keeping the information of customers and clients private:

Install Anti-Malware Software

It's easy to assume that your employees know to never open phishing emails. However, the Verizon 2016 Data Breach Investigations Report found that 30 percent of employees opened phishing emails, a 7 percent increase from 2015. Since phishing attacks involve installing malware on the employee's computer when the link is clicked, it's essential to have anti-malware software installed on all devices and the network. Since phishing attacks often target specific SMB employee roles, use the position-specific tactics outlined in the Entreprenuer.com article "5 Types of Employees Often Targeted by Phishing Attacks" as part of your training.

Don't Collect What You Don't Need

The more valuable information you have, the bigger a target you might be. Avoid using social security numbers or other personal information for customer identification. Opt instead for log in identification and passwords. More layers of identification help keep attackers from being able to simulate users. Consider deleting personal information that you don't really need.

If You Collect It, Protect It

Follow reasonable security measures to ensure that customers' and employees' personal information is protected from inappropriate and unauthorized access.

Scan All New Devices

Be sure to scan all USB and other devices before they are attached to your network.

Use A Firewall

One of the first lines of defense in a cyber-attack is a firewall. The Federal Communications Commission (FCC) recommends that all SMBs set up a firewall to provide a barrier between your data and cybercriminals. In addition to the standard external firewall, many companies are starting to install internal firewalls to provide additional protection. It's also important that employees working from home install a firewall on their home network as well. Consider providing firewall software and support for home networks to ensure compliance.

Educate Employees

Employees are often the handlers of customer data. They therefore need to be kept up-to-date on how to protect that information to make sure it does not accidentally land in the wrong hands. They should be educated about the newest fraud schemes and urged to employ best practices such as not responding to or opening attachments or clicking suspicious links in unsolicited email messages.

Have A Strong Privacy Policy

Customers need to know that you are protecting their information. Make sure you have a policy they can refer to explaining how you are keeping personal information safe. Make sure you are straightforward with customers about the consumer data you collect and what you do with it. Being honest with them will help you build consumer trust and show you value their data and are working to protect it.

Enforce Safe Password Practices

Yes, employees find changing passwords to be a pain. However, the Verizon 2016 Data Breach Investigations Report found that 63 percent of data breaches happened due to lost, stolen or weak passwords. According to the Keeper Security and Ponemon Institute Report, 65 percent of SMBs with password policies do not enforce it. In today's BYOD world, it's essential that all employee devices accessing the company network be password protected.

In the Business Daily article "Cybersecurity: A Small Business Guide," Bill Carey, vice president of marketing and business development at Siber Systems, recommended that employees be required to use passwords with upper- and lowercase letters, numbers and symbols. He says that SMBs should require all passwords to be changed every 60 to 90 days.

Regularly Back Up All Data

While it's important to prevent as many attacks as possible, it is still possible to be breached regardless of your precautions. The SBA recommends backing up word processing documents, electronic spreadsheets, databases, financial files, human resources files, and accounts receivable/payable files. Be sure to also back up all data stored on the cloud. Make sure that backups are stored in a separate location in case of fire or flood. To ensure that you will have the latest backup if you ever need it, check your backup regularly to ensure that it is functioning correctly.

Use Multifactor Identification

Regardless of your preparation, an employee will likely make a security mistake that can compromise your data. In the PC Week article "10 Cyber Security Steps Your Small Business Should Take Right Now," Matt Littleton, East Regional Director of Cybersecurity and Azure Infrastructure Services at Microsoft, says using the multi-factor identification settings on most major network and email products is simple to do and provides an extra layer of protection. He recommends using employees' cell numbers as a second form, since it is unlikely a thief will have both the PIN and the password.

Keep A Clean Machine

Having the latest security software, web browser and operating system are the best defenses against viruses, malware and other online threats. Many software programs will automatically connect and update to defend against known risks. Turn on automatic updates if that's an available option.

Protect Against Mobile Device Risks

Smartphones, tablets and laptops can add to employee flexibility and productivity, but they can also be repositories of sensitive information, which, if lost, can harm your customers and your business. Impress upon employees and other partners the importance of keeping these devices secure from loss or theft. At the same time, stress that not reporting such an incident, if it happens, is worse.

Know What You Are Protecting

Be aware of all the personal information you have, where you are storing it, how you are using it and who has access to it. Understand the kind of assets you have and why a hacker might pursue them. "You cannot protect what you don't know about," Sundaresan said.

Don't Underestimate The Threat

In one survey conducted by the Alliance, 85 percent of small business owners believe larger enterprises are more targeted than they are. In reality, there have been cases where small businesses have lost hundreds of thousands of dollars to cybercriminals.

HOW TO HANDLE YOUR CUSTOMERS AND PROVIDE EXEMPLARY CUSTOMER SERVICES

Your company's most vital asset is its customers, so you need to make sure you're dealing with your customers properly. Without them, you would not, and could not, exist in business. Sure, you can attract new customers with unique products, free gifts, or reducing your prices; but if you're not creating relationships with them, they're not going to return or recommend you.

Sometimes it can be challenging to build those relationships. The questions you get asked in a customer facing role can be in equal parts interesting, monotonous, funny and challenging. The key is to make each customer feel welcome and helped.

Here are tips for dealing with customers and delivering excellent customer service:

Stay Calm

Difficult as it is sometimes, it is important to stay calm. Your calming approach will help your customer stay calm too. They will feel like you're in control of the situation and that you can help solve their problem.

Take Them Seriously

Make customers feel important and appreciated. No matter how ridiculous a question may sound to you; it's important to the customer. If they feel like they're being laughed at, or spoken down to, they will not purchase anything. Customers can be very sensitive and will know whether or not you really care about them.

Acknowledge Your Limits

Yes is a powerful word but if you're unable to fulfil a request: know your limits. You can't be everything to everyone. If you don't think you can fulfil the request, help them find an alternate remedy. Whether that remedy is your business or another, they will appreciate the extra mile you went to help them, and will recommend your business to their network.

Identify and Anticipate Needs

Most customer needs are emotional rather than logical. The more you know your customers, the better you become at anticipating their needs. Communicate regularly so that you're aware of problems or upcoming needs.

Suggest Solutions

Have a menu of calming remedies which you and your employees can use. Whether it's purely a refund or return, or if it's coupons or a free service. By agreeing in advance the scenarios where you will provide these remedies, and how much you're willing to spend, you will be able to speak calmer and more confidently when offering the solution.

Appreciate the Power of "Yes"

Always look for ways to help your customers. When they have a request (as long as it is reasonable) tell them that you can do it. Figure out how afterwards. Look for ways to make doing business with you easy. Always do what you say you're going to do.

Listen to Customers

Sometimes, customers just need to know that you're listening. If they're confused or have a problem, by lending a listening ear, you're showing that you care and that you're not dismissing them.

Apologize

When something goes wrong, apologize. It's amazing how calming the words "I'm sorry" can be. Don't engage in fault-finding or laying blame, but let them know you're sorry they had a problem. Deal with the problem immediately and let the customer know what you have done.

Be Available

Customer service is no longer just about face-to-face contact and telephone. If you're working in an industry or marketplace where customers are constantly online, you need to amend your service delivery to incorporate that. It does not need to be a dedicated helpdesk Twitter handle, simply make sure you respond promptly and informatively to clients on your main business Facebook page or to your Twitter account.

Get Regular Feedback

Feedback is a great way to grow both your business and your skills. Provide ways for customers to give feedback, whether it's a follow up email or phone call, a suggestions box or something more fun and innovative.

WAYS TO GET YOUR STARTUP FUNDED

Here's an overview of typical sources of financing for start-ups:

Personal investment

When starting a business, your first investor should be yourself—either with your own cash or with collateral on your assets. This proves to investors and bankers that you have a long-term commitment to your project and that you are ready to take risks.

Business incubators

Business incubators (or "accelerators") generally focus on the high-tech sector by providing support for new businesses in various stages of development. However, there are also local economic development incubators, which are focused on areas such as job creation, revitalization and hosting and sharing services.

Commonly, incubators will invite future businesses and other fledgling companies to share their premises, as well as their administrative, logistical and technical resources. For example, an incubator might share the use of its laboratories so that a new business can develop and test its products more cheaply before beginning production.

Generally, the incubation phase can last up to two years. Once the product is ready, the business usually leaves the incubator's premises to enter its industrial production phase and is on its own.

Businesses that receive this kind of support often operate within state-of-the-art sectors such as biotechnology, information technology, multimedia, or industrial technology.

MaRS – an innovation hub in Toronto – has a selective list of business incubators in Canada, plus links to other resources on its website.

Angel investors

Although these terms are often used interchangeably, angel investors differ from VCs.

While angel investors can take an equity share of your startup in exchange for their investment, their funding can also be exchanged for convertible debt.

It's not uncommon for these investors to be entrepreneurs or former entrepreneurs themselves.

Although money is their motivation, they are more likely to be genuinely interested in your business as well as the growth and development of particular industries.

If you find the right angel investor, you may benefit from their expert advice and management skills.

It's more common for angel investors to supply funding to businesses when they are still in the early stages, whereas VCs typically look to get involved a little bit later.

Unlike a VC firm that has a committee and advisors working together, an angel investor may make a decision on their own.

They may simply like your plan, trust your goals, and believe that your business will be successful.

That's why it's important for you to be able to articulate your business plan well.

A short meeting over coffee or lunch with an angel investor might be all it takes to get them on board to fund your startup.

Crowdfunding

Take advantage of the resources available to you online.

You can use crowdfunding websites to raise capital.

While most people think of Kickstarter when it comes to these platforms, there are some alternative websites you can consider as well.

Here are a few popular choices for startup companies:

- AngelList
- CircleUp
- CrowdFunder
- Fundable

Government grants and subsidies

Government agencies provide financing such as grants and subsidies that may be available to your business. The Canada Business Network website provides a comprehensive listing of various government programs at the federal and provincial level.

HOW MUCH DO DROPSHIPPERS MAKE AND HOW SOON

Success stories from AliDropShip

This [AliDropship](#) forum contributor runs a general store aimed on buyers from the Phillipines, The USA, and Brazil, and the average daily amount of sales exceeds $3,000. The road to success was quite bumpy, but with some courage, confidence, and faith (and Google AdWords) it became possible to achieve these incredible results.

Another forum poster, Rewall, spend about a year learning as much about dropshipping as possible, and in about 2 months, the income of his 2 stores hit the mark of $26,700. Facebook Ads did the magic!

Pirn from Estonia also used the AliDropship forum to share his success story, but our team got so impressed with his achievements that we asked him for a blog interview right away. It's quite understandable: having no background experience, this EU dropshipper managed to achieve an average dropshipping income exceeding $10,000 per month!

Similar results can be seen in the store of Otto who also runs his business in the Baltic states area. Otto runs 4 dropshipping stores at once, and the top billing one generates over $13,000 on a monthly basis.

The list goes on and on; if you're curious, feel free to read the story of Rahul from India whose 4 stores went from 0 to $12,000 in 5 months, or the story of Martin from the Netherlands who made over 4,100 EUR in 30 days, or the story of Yan from France who went from 0 to $1358.41 in 52 days despite zero experience – we've got plenty of such testimonials.

What conclusion can we draw from all these numbers?

Dropshipping puts no limits on your profits

As you can see, each and every particular dropshipping store owner has a dramatically different level of income. Still, there is a striking similarity: all the owners are not constrained by any 'requirements' or 'limits' on amount of conducted sales, pricing markup, overall revenue, etc. Whatever the income amount is, it's all yours. That's exactly the thing that makes you highly motivated to keep developing the store, and aim higher.

No obstacles are significant enough to put your dropshipping income at risk

Life goes pretty fast, and lots of events can directly or indirectly influence your dropshipping business performance.

For example, Mousslim's success story reveals that he has unknowingly launched his business during the Chinese New Year (the time when the majority of AliExpress sellers go on a vacation that can last for up to several weeks). Fortunately, he still managed to run his business with the maximum efficiency possible, and that's a really awesome feature of dropshipping business model. With due preparation, your store will still make enough money no matter what the circumstances are: Chinese New Year, Black Friday, or your own vacation.

There is more to dropshipping business than just money

This idea is expressed very clearly in Otto's success story: on numerous occasions, he mentions that there is a huge difference between running your own store and working for somebody. In Otto's opinion, the fear of having to work for someone else's benefit is the most powerful motivator to run your own venture.

REASONS OF DROPSHIPPING FAILURES

Below is a comprehensive list of these dropshipping failures. It is as detailed as possible and provide solutions to all the problems.

Lack of Patience & Persistence

Most dropshippers just don't have the patience to start a dropshipping store. So, if you aren't patient enough then my advice is to start forex trading instead because that's where you can earn instant money (or even lose it). Patience and persistence are not only required in dropshipping but for any business. And, if you are just starting out with dropshipping then it is a prerequisite.

High Prices of Dropshipping Products

Most of the visitors of a dropshipping store will search for the same product at another store just to compare the prices. This is because customers are now aware that most stores are selling the same products so they can easily get better deals elsewhere. If they think they can get the same product at a low price somewhere else, then they will leave the store.

So, it is better to keep a lower price of the product that you are selling on your dropshipping store while still staying profitable. You will have to learn to balance the both.

Bad Customer Support

Another reason why most dropshippers fail is that they are not good managers of the dropshipping stores. Dropshipping doesn't end when the customer's product is dispatched. You will still have to reply to their queries and stay connected with them until they are satisfied with their products.

In the example I described above, one dropshipper that was selling clothes from wholesalers and didn't realize that clothes have the highest return rate. Since he wasn't able to cope with that, he failed.

Lack of Investment/Resources

Though dropshipping doesn't require a lot of investment if you are just starting out for the first time then you need to keep a budget in mind. Let's say you have just started your first store, so you need to keep at least $300-$400 for advertisements. If you lack even this amount of investment then it is better not to go into dropshipping until you have saved enough.

Selection of Wrong Platform

One reason most dropshippers fail is that they are using the wrong platform to market their dropshipping stores and products. Some of the most prominent channels to market your dropshipping products are Facebook Ads, Google Adwords, and Bing Ads. If dropshippers have found products that are already selling in high volumes on other shopping stores then you only have to market them. If you are still failing, then it can be because you are not using the right platform.

The best solution to this problem is to use multiple platforms to market the product and the one that provides the most ROI, use it further on.

Selecting the Wrong Niche

The first reason for the dropshipping failures is because of the wrong niche selection. A friend of mine wanted to target US traffic with one of his dropshipping stores. He chose a niche clothing line and started promoting the products in the USA. Too bad, he didn't even receive a single order.

Inconsistency in Managing Business

Most dropshippers are just wantrepreneurs. They are only interested in starting a business and not in keeping it alive. In short, they are inconsistent. Same happens with dropshipping. In fact, business magazine Forbes says that every 8/10 businesses fail in less than a year. And, one major reason for the failure is inconsistency or a lack of planning.

Unattractive Website Design

Here is an analogy to understand why dropshipping failures occur due to a bad UI. There are two stores: one is air-conditioned and has automated sliding doors for the visitors. Inside, a gorgeous looking hostess welcomes everyone, while escorting them to the products they want to buy.

Pick the Right Model for Your Dropshipping Store

He was depressed but not ready to quit. So, he started targeting the same product in Ukraine and received more than a 100 orders in a single day.

Point to note here: Targeting a wrong country with a particular niche can destroy your business. The best strategy to cope out of it is to test, test, and test.

Delayed Shipping

In America, especially after Amazon started prime delivery, people now prefer ordering products from it because they can get theirs in just a single day. However, dropshipping is usually from China, so the minimum shipping time is at least 20 days. People can't wait this long to get their products. Another reason most dropshippers fail is that they don't order products through ePacket. This means the buyer won't get a tracking number, decreasing his trust in the store.

DROPSHIPPING MISTAKES TO AVOID

Common mistakes that should be avoided when picking a product for dropshipping:

Do not base your choice of product on what your likes and dislikes are.

Always base your product decision on facts, research, due diligence and evaluating and validating the market's demand.

Do not sell knock-off or "true copies".

Not only is this a cheap gimmick that won't necessarily get you anywhere with customers, but it is also illegal in most countries! Avoid these type of products so you can avoid the hassle or dropship products from reliable and official merchandisers such as MXED.

Don't just hop onto the bandwagon.

"If everyone is selling it, I should too," isn't always the right reason to pick a product. The market for trending products is typically very saturated so there will be high levels of competition. If trending products are something you want to pursue then make sure to conduct thorough research into the rise and fall of the trend so you know what to expect from consumer interests. Check out a tool like Google Trends to help evaluate trends.

DROPSHIPPING TIPS TO SKYROCKET YOUR SALES IN 2019

Dropshipping is undoubtedly a great business model for any entrepreneur looking to get into ecommerce. It is easy to start, cost effective, low risk, and offers incredible flexibility in terms of time, and what you can do.

Easy as it may sound, drop shipping is a serious business for serious entrepreneurs. New marketers often make common mistakes that see their business taken to the cleaners not long after launching.

There are some things, when done correctly can turn your small store into a recognizable online brand. But, what are these things that new and experience marketers need to pay attention to?

Know Your Niche More than Your Customers

The first mistake new marketers make is to choose the wrong niche when going into dropshipping. Often, people pick a niche based on what other marketers are saying is going to sell.

Well, not everything sells like hotcake, and those that are in demand have already flooded the market. Prudent sellers go for the niche they are familiar with. Alas, how do you sell a product you are not interested in? Don't be surprised if you find yourself selling to the wrong people!

You'll agree with me that it is necessary that you sell products that you are passionate about as well as those that you have knowledge about.

If you are crazy about children and the environment, but at the same time have no idea what kids crave on different stages, it will certainly help to take a few child psychology and children behavioral pattern courses. Otherwise, you cannot launch a well considered, well targeted kids store.

Find the right supplier for your business

The suppliers you partner with are crucial to a successful dropship business. They are the ones who fulfill orders on your behalf, and the reputation and image of your brand are completely dependent on them delivering high-quality and well-packaged goods on time.

If the suppliers you partner with do not have strict quality standards and do not adhere to the shipping timelines promised by you to your customers, it will ultimately affect your credibility, trustworthiness and reputation.

Conduct Competitive Intelligence Will Make Your Business Much Easier

The fuss about ecommerce as an easy way of starting a business and making money has created a lot of competition to the point that only the most unique sellers really enjoy the bounty. Competitive intelligence often reveals insightful tricks and tips that your competition is using to get ahead of the game.

Keeping an eye on the competition discloses their strength and weaknesses. This goes a long way to help you become an even better seller.

Plenty of competitor information is publically available and can be obtained through legal means. So, you don't have to peep through office windows nor have their computers hacked.

Here's what you can do to keep tabs on your competition:

- Check their websites
- Visit their social media profiles
- Order their products
- Go to industry trade shows
- Go through competitor customer reviews
- Subscribe to their mailing lists

Order Product Samples

A good tip is to order samples of the products you want to sell. This will not only give you a first-hand feel of what your customers experience, but you can also assess your suppliers, their packaging and delivery time, and make any changes to improve the experience for your customers.

When you order samples, it gives you the chance to handle your products. You can click unique product pictures or make interesting product videos as marketing collateral.

You're also assured of product quality, and if you're not satisfied you can easily change suppliers before it hurts your brand.

Avoid Under-Pricing Your Products

Take profit margins into consideration when you decide on which products to sell. Factor in overheads like office supplies, staff and marketing expenses. Do not undercut your prices only because your competitors are doing the same, however tempting that might be!

If you offer quality products and price them fairly, keeping within the market-value, you will find customers. Swift customer service, a hassle-free returns and refund policy, personalized packaging etc, all add to an enhanced shopping experience, and customers will not mind paying an extra buck for it.

Do not skimp on quality to increase your margins, it will get you nowhere in the long run, and you will be one of the many dropship start-ups that have disappeared into oblivion.

Work on increasing the average order value to make higher profits from every order. Ensure your eCommerce platform has marketing features like up-sell and cross sell suggestions.

While the norm is to go for products with a high profit margin, there are products with a low profit margin, like IT for example, that will generate profit if you sell larger volumes. Selling high-ticket IT products is also a really profitable niche and one that is not explored to its full potential.

Rev Up Your Customer Service Will Keep Your Customers Coming Back

Customer service is all about conversational commerce. A great customer service is a dropshippers best tool. With a remarkable customer service, you can beat even the giant ecommerce competition in your industry.

Reving up your customer service is all about making the customer feel respected, valued, and important. Don't lure in the customer just to push sales. Rather try to build a solid customer base.

An important thing to note about customer service for dropshippers is that the customers have to see that you actually care for their wants and needs.

Here is how to be a responsible dropshipper who is responsible for their customers' needs.

- Educate
- Communicate

- Build relationships with clients
- Respond to both positive and negative feedback

Use a proper eCommerce platform for your dropshipping store

The eCommerce platform you choose will determine whether your dropship business will be smooth-sailing or run through choppy waters.

Yes, it is one of THE most important decisions you will have to make. There are innumerable eCommerce platforms at your disposal, each offering more or less similar features and capabilities.

Choosing one out of the many will depend on the products you want to sell and the market you want to target. There are some features that you cannot compromise on. Stick to your guns, and you will find an eCommerce platform that will cater to all your needs.

A few things that are a must-have in a good eCommerce platform are:

Integrations with the distributors' product feed:

Direct integrations with distributors' product feeds will make your life a lot easier. This takes away the effort and time required to manually upload products, click images and write product description.

Integrations with popular CRMs, ERPs and accounting software:

Ensures a seamless and smooth workflow and eliminates repetition of processes.

Automation of freight and taxes:

Automating freight calculations on pre-set rules makes checkout a lot quicker, which, to be honest, is the end game. Taxation laws differ in different countries and states. You do not want legal repercussions for defaulting on taxes. Automation ensures that you're always in the clear, and customers trust your brand as there is transparency.

Scalability:

The eCommerce platform you choose should grow as your business grows. Many eCommerce platforms have charges as you scale, take these into account as you build the road-map for your business. The ideal would be an eCommerce platform that allows you to scale without additional costs. Research well and you will find one that suits your niche and product.

Mobile friendliness:

This is a no-brainer; mobile shopping is on the rise and your eCommerce store should adapt and be responsive on various devices.

Security:

A lot of data is online these days and data security is a concern when shopping online. Add trust badges to your eCommerce store and ensure that it is PCI compliant.

Create Custom Product Images

Being unique sales. Creating custom content sets you apart from the rest of the online sellers. This is a great way to increase traffic to your webstore.

If possible, use your own product images. Capture the different angles that your customers might be interested to view. Using custom product images sets your brand apart because most other sellers are using the same old stock photos.

Make sure you produce quality images and it will up your game.

Make Shipping Times Very Clear

Consumers buy online for the convenience it offers. But there are various factors that mar the online shopping experience for a consumer. Uncertainty over shipping and delivery times is one.

Always be clear about the delivery times and offer tracking information to customers. It will enhance the buying experience for them and increase the trust they have in your brand.

Create An Amazing Offer

Offers and deals are what's driving people online these days, and if you want to get in the eCommerce limelight, that is what you should do.

Sales and bundles motivate consumers to buy, create enticing offers, or bundle products together. Bundling is when you create a package of similar products and offer a better price for the group than you would for one.

For example, if one notepad costs $5, you can create a bundle of 10 notepads at $45. The saving motivates a customer to buy, and they associate your brand as having good bargains and promotions.

Upsell, cross-sell, bundle and offer deals and promotions, anything to get the customer to pull that credit card out!

Put Effort into Your Website's Experience

A successful online store owner values customer experience. You have to put effort into creating a web store with a clean interface, easy navigation, quality product images, detailed product description, clear return policies, and a smooth checkout process.

As you optimize your web store for the user ensure also that SEO is clean.

Below are some critical aspect your web store should have:

- About and Contact page
- Professional logo
- Featured product
- Privacy policy
- Return and exchange policies
- Shipping process details
- FAQs page
- Size guide (where applicable)

FREQUENTLY ASKED QUESTION

Are you looking to start a dropshipping business but have some questions and concerns holding you back?

Get all your questions answered in this comprehensive dropshipping FAQ. I hope you'll be able to clear up some of your concerns and start your dropshipping journey.

What is dropshipping?

Dropshipping is a type of eCommerce business where you as the seller of a product, does not keep goods in your warehouse but transfers the customer's orders and shipment details to the dropship suppliers who now ships the goods directly to your customers.

Is dropshipping legal?

Nothing is illegal about dropshipping. In fact, it is the same as a normal retail business. The only difference is that your supplier is handling the shipping for you. There is no law against the dropshipping business model.

However, some eCommerce platform may prevent their seller to dropship products in their platform such as Amazon. i.e if you plan to sell a product that you dropship in Amazon, then your account may get banned from Amazon.

But if you are planning to dropship with your own eCommerce store (which you really should), then there are no restrictions at all. You have full control and ownership to your own eCommerce store.

Is dropshipping worth it in 2020?

The answer is a definite YES! It is still a very profitable business model. But this doesn't mean it is a sure win business.

Honestly, there is no sure win business or business that you can earn a lot without doing much work. But with the right strategy and guidance, you can increase your success rate tremendously.

Are the products from suppliers and manufacturers are made by junks or low ⍰uality raw materials?

I need to say it should depends on the suppliers and manufacturers that you are cooperating with.

Therefore, you need to partner with a reliable drop shipping platform which can provide you higher quality products. It should be better to do it with platform that has professional QC team for checking product quality such as Chinabrands.

How about the delivery between regions with long distances? I don't want to receive a negative review or feedback because of the late delivery or logistic issues.

This is the main reason why drop shipping retailers are prefer cooperating with a reliable platform such as Chinabrands. They should provides high quality delivery services, and its global warehousing services should be more convenience for deliver merchandises between regions or countries.

Can we do drop shipping business worldwide?

Of course yes. Drop shipping requires lower start-up capital, which means it should be easier for retailers to expand their business to the world.

Do I need to built up a store first before selling?

Basically, you don't need to built up your own store before join in drop shipping business. But it should be better to build up your own stores even brands, and it is helpful for strengthen your brand awareness among customers.

Should I need to pay for the merchandises first before deliver it to my customers?

The answer is NO if you are working with drop shipping. Suppliers or manufacturers should deliver merchandises directly to your end-customers. You only need to pay for the product once the order placed on your store.

How can I find the suppliers that I need, cause I'm beginner for drop shipping?

You can join a drop shipping platform like Chinabrands, they should provide a bunch of available suppliers for your selection.

How can I make profits for drop shipping business?

Of course you can make more profits as you are selling much more products. Moreover, you can do marketing operation such as promotion, advertisement for attracting your targeted customers. The prior market research should be helpful for your marketing strategies.

What is the profit margin then? Can I do it for my living?

Basically, the profit margins are depend on the sales and policies in different business partners such as drop shipping platform or suppliers. As the recent research shows that the average profit margin of drop shipping business is approx 15-30%.

Should I pay for taxes if I deliver merchandises between countries or regions?

Yes, you should pay for it if you delivering it globally. The tax fees are different which depend on your countries and the final destination, and also the product values.

Do I need to purchase multiple products for my store inventories?

No, you don't need to. It should be fine that you don't have inventories because most of drop shipping platform or website should manage inventories for you.

It is so annoying for uploading and downloading so many product description on drop shipping store, any technologies supports for deal with it?

As I know that there are some drop shipping platform like Chinabrands should built up its API system, which means you can bulk upload and download product description and images on API system.

I'm a beginner to do drop shipping business, what is the most basic drop shipping process?

Drop shipping is a retail method that should be easier for understanding and implementing. The basic drop shipping process should be a cycle which start from Preparation, and end with Searching for new niches.

Anything I can do during the process of selling? Or any other ways for me to promote my drop shipping store?

You can't just waiting for your customers when you are selling your products. You need to try your best to promote your drop shipping store by doing market research, advertising, promotion and so on.

Can I selling products on different websites? I need to figure out which one is better for me.

Yes, you can. But it is difficult for managing so many account at the same time. So it is better to join a drop shipping platform like Chinabrands which can be helpful for your account management on different drop shipping website such as Amazon and eBay.

Any minimum consumption or number of products?

With drop shipping business model, there is no minimum consumption or number of products. For most of drop shipping websites, they setting up a minimum order number only for wholesaling. Therefore, it doesn't matter if you want to buy it even a single unit.

Any requirements for product description and images before I upload it on my store?

There are different requirements between drop shipping websites. For example, Amazon require sellers to upload product images with white color background. Therefore, a quick tip here, it should be better for sellers to cooperate with a drop shipping platform like Chinabrands. They can allows members to bulk download and upload high-quality products images and its description from their websites.

There are some problems that I can't deal with such as disputes with customers or supplying issues, what should I do if I must to deal with it?

The first thing you must to do is figure out what happened whatever disputes or supplying issues. And then you should contacting with staffs or customer service team to let your partners know about it. The drop shipping platform or your suppliers should make responses as quick as possible, that should requires you to make a conversation with your customers. Remember, conversation and negotiation is the best way for dealing with most of problems for your drop shipping business. Try to figure out the reasons, and solve it with your partners.

CONCLUSION

Drop shipping is definitely an option you want to consider if you're planning to start an online retail business without all the hassles of inventory and product delivery. If you evaluate the above advantages carefully, you'll realize that drop shipping is undoubtedly a viable option for the small-business retailer. Large retailers, on the other hand, will have enough resources like capital to use the wholesaling model for their business.

SUMMARY

Getting started and how to dropship

Now we're fully aware of the pros and cons of setting up a dropshipping business, it's decision time!

- If you have existing WordPress skills and are after a business where you primarily add value through branding and marketing, then go ahead. If you want to spend time making your product, this probably isn't for you. You could always start a blog if the WordPress product space really doesn't appeal.

- If you're okay with the caveats and excited about building a great store, brand, and customer experience, then let's go!

On the assumption you're still reading because you're at the very least curious, let's move on to the best approach to how to dropship and setting up your dropshipping business: from honing in on your winning business idea to sourcing your supplier and finding your first customers.

Market research: Find a niche & choose your product

This is the bare-bones foundation of your business, so you'd best make it solid!

You need a niche: something your store will focus on. Think "bespoke coffee store" rather than "Amazon competitor". Ideally, your niche is where you already have expert knowledge. Or perhaps it's a topic/product which is relatively undiscovered and under-utilized: ideally, a combination of both!

You'll have a much higher chance of success if you have a comparative advantage over the competition – even if it's just your expert knowledge. "Expert knowledge" in a topic or type of product that you're really passionate about. An existing hobby, for example.

Perhaps you love sourcing highly unusual, attractive artwork and you also enjoy photographing birds. Or you're a new mother, but don't want to give up your passion for golf. These are both great niches because they sit at the intersection of two categories. If you're an expert in both, you've got an immediate competitive advantage. This sort of an approach is a great way to learn how to dropship.

Sourcing the right eCommerce provider and dropshipping supplier

Whether you already have an eCommerce store or learning how to start a dropshipping business from scratch; it's absolutely essential to find a good match between your eCommerce provider and dropshipping supplier.

These services will be sharing information day in, day out and compatibility issues can cause untold problems. Shopify, for example, has its own dedicated dropshipping app, Oberlo. It's pretty impressive, but you're stuck inside the Shopify ecosystem.

AliExpress can be a key part of your journey with how to start a dropshipping business.

You should do your due diligence when choosing a marketplace, and remember you're choosing a marketplace and need a supplier within that marketplace. You'll want to know about customer support, shipping fees, and which channels you can sell through. Other popular options are YouDroop and DropShix. We'll proceed with AliExpress here for the range of products and WooCommerce integration, but go for the marketplace with the best options for your niche.

Finding your first customers: Getting eyes on the prize

Your dropshipping store needs visitors and customers to thrive – you won't learn how to dropship without customers! To start with, keep things simple and focus in on marketing channels most likely to attract sales to your website.

You should think about possible marketing channels, and if you have access or skills for an unusual or unorthodox channel, then do that! That's a great way of getting your first customers. Here, however, we'll recommend content marketing because it's scalable' roots, so you're likely able to do a decent job.

The key things to remember here are:

- Create really good content that answers unanswered questions related to your products, or answers already-answered questions better than is being done currently.
- Have a target keyword in mind for each post.
- Commit to a couple of months of content marketing. It takes time to work.

You can add things like tracking your search rankings, using UTM codes to track the sales results from each post, and building an email list, but those are things to look at once this is working (which you'll know as you'll have sales!). The key is to provide real value and useful information, which will keep customers returning to your site.

Try this out, and make sure to strike the right balance between committing for the right amount of time and tweaking strategy when required. This is a fantastic way to build out customers for your store and ultimately learn how to dropship.

Success stories: learn how to start a dropshipping business from the pros

Let's check out some dropshipping for eCommerce success stories! This is a really exciting field, so we'll see what we can learn from those already running successful dropshipping companies.

www.ingramcontent.com/pod-product-compliance
Lightning Source LLC
Chambersburg PA
CBHW021811170526
45157CB00007B/2544